Ultimate Egg Cookbook

Breakfast Casseroles, Quiches, Omelets & More!

S. L. Watson

DEDICATION

To egg lover's everywhere!

CONTENTS

INTRODUCTION

Eggs are a budget conscious and nutritious food. Eggs are served at breakfast, brunch, lunch and dinner. Included are over 240 recipes featuring eggs. Included are casseroles, stratas, quiches, omelets, frittatas, deviled eggs and more. The recipes include a wide variety of vegetables, cheeses and flavors for most any taste.

Most egg casseroles and quiches are easy to make. Most everyone loves a hearty breakfast casserole. You can make most quiches without a pie crust. Be sure to spray your pie pan with non stick cooking spray before filling. The recipes are easy to prepare and do not require special cooking skills or ingredients.

1 EGGS, OMELETS & FRITTATAS

My family will eat eggs at most any meal. After a busy day, breakfast for dinner is on the menu. Omelets and frittatas are a quick easy meal and you can use up leftover meats and vegetables to make them.

How to Cook Eggs for Breakfast

Southern Fried Egg: Place 2 teaspoons butter in a non stick or cast iron skillet over medium low heat. If your skillet is too hot, the egg white will crisp and be tough. When the butter melts, gently break four eggs, one at a time, into the skillet. Cook for 1-2 minutes or until the egg whites are no longer runny around the yolk. Turn the egg over and cook an additional 30 seconds to 1 minute. This will make the perfect fried egg with a runny yolk. If you do not want a runny yolk, cook the egg for an additional 1 minute on each side.

Scrambled Eggs: The key to perfect scrambled eggs is slow cooking. In a small bowl, place 2 eggs per person. Add 1 teaspoon milk for every two eggs. Add salt and pepper to taste and whisk until the eggs are well combined or about 30 seconds.

In a skillet over low heat, melt 1-2 teaspoons butter. When the butter melts, pour the eggs into the skillet. Let the bottom of the eggs set before stirring. Stir around the skillet to scramble the eggs. Cook until the eggs are set but still moist. This takes about 5 minutes depending upon the amount of eggs in your skillet.

Oven eggs: This is my favorite way to eat eggs. It is so easy and the possibilities are endless. The eggs puff up and are very creamy. Very easy to do on busy mornings. Place the eggs in the oven while you are getting ready for work or school and breakfast will be done in a jiffy.

Preheat the oven to 350°. Using a cast iron skillet or non stick skillet made for the oven, place one tablespoon butter in the skillet. Place the skillet in the oven to melt the butter. Remove the skillet from the oven when the butter has melted.

In a mixing bowl, add 6 eggs. Add 3 tablespoons milk and season with salt and black pepper if desired. Whisk the eggs for one minute. At this point, you can add 1/2 to 1 cup cooked bacon, sausage, ham, cheese or vegetables if desired. Pour the eggs into the hot skillet. Place the skillet back in the oven and cook for 15-20 minutes or until the eggs are set in the center.

The eggs will puff up during the cooking process and shrink when you remove them from the oven. If you have leftovers, place them in the refrigerator for two days. Reheat leftovers in the microwave.

Poached Eggs: Fill a sauce pan or skillet with 3" water. Bring the water to a boil and then reduce the heat to medium low. The water should not be boiling but simmering. Do not add the eggs to the water until the water is simmering.

Crack a cold egg into a small ramekin. Hold the ramekin close to the water and gently let the egg slide into the water. Cook until the egg whites are completely set and the yolk begins thicken. This takes about 4 minutes on my stove. Remove the egg from the water with a slotted spoon.

You can cook several eggs at a time. Repeat the steps with the amount of eggs you need to cook. I would not add more than 4 eggs at a time.

Sausage Cheddar Frittata

Makes 8 servings

10 eggs
1/2 cup whole milk
1/2 tsp. salt
1/2 tsp. black pepper
2 tbs. unsalted butter
12 oz. pork sausage, cooked and crumbled
1 cup shredded cheddar cheese

In a mixing bowl, add the eggs, milk, salt and black pepper. Whisk until well combined. Add the butter to a 12" oven proof skillet over medium heat. When the butter melts, remove the skillet from the heat. Add half the eggs to the skillet. Sprinkle the sausage and cheddar cheese over the eggs. Pour the remaining eggs over the sausage.

Preheat the oven to 350°. Bake for 15 minutes or until the eggs are set in the center. Remove the skillet from the oven and serve.

Ham & Pepper Frittata

Makes 2 servings

4 eggs
2 tbs. whole milk
1/8 tsp. black pepper
1/8 tsp. salt
1/4 cup chopped orange bell pepper
2 green onions, thinly sliced
1/2 tsp. vegetable oil
1/2 cup cubed cooked ham
1/4 cup shredded cheddar cheese

Preheat the oven to the broiler position. In a small bowl, add the eggs, milk, black pepper and salt. Whisk until combined. In an 8" oven proof skillet over medium heat, add the orange bell pepper, green onions and vegetable oil. Saute for 4 minutes. Add the ham to the skillet. Saute for 2 minutes.

Add the eggs to the skillet. Do not stir. Place a lid on the skillet. Cook for 4 minutes or until the frittata is almost set. Remove from the heat and sprinkle the cheddar cheese over the top. Leave the lid off the skillet and broil for 2-3 minutes or until the frittata is set in the center. Remove from the oven and serve.

Tex Mex Ham & Egg Frittata

Makes 2 servings

1 cup chopped cooked ham
1/2 cup chopped onion
2 tbs. vegetable oil
2 cups frozen shredded hashbrowns, thawed
2 eggs
2 tbs. whole milk
Salt and black pepper to taste
1/2 cup shredded cheddar cheese
2 tbs. chunky salsa

In a skillet over medium heat, add the ham, onion and 1 tablespoon vegetable oil. Saute for 5 minutes or until the ham is browned. Remove the ham and onion from the skillet and drain on paper towels.

Add 1 tablespoon vegetable oil to the skillet. When the oil is hot, add the hashbrowns. Stir frequently and cook for 5 minutes or until the hashbrowns are tender and browned.

In a small bowl, add the eggs and milk. Whisk until combined and season to taste with salt and black pepper. Add the ham and onion to the bowl. Whisk until combined and pour over the hashbrowns. Do not stir.

As the edges of the frittata set, gently lift the edges to allow the uncooked eggs to run underneath. Cook about 4-5 minutes or until the eggs are completely set. Sprinkle the cheddar cheese over the top. Remove the skillet from the heat and spoon the salsa over the top.

Caramelized Mushroom & Onion Frittata

Makes 4 servings

1 lb. sliced fresh mushrooms
1 cup chopped onion
3 tbs. unsalted butter
3 tbs. olive oil
1 shallot, chopped
1 garlic clove, minced
1/2 cup shredded cheddar cheese
1/4 cup shredded Parmesan cheese
8 eggs
3 tbs. heavy whipping cream
1/4 tsp. salt
1/4 tsp. black pepper

In a 10" oven proof skillet over medium heat, add the mushrooms, onions, butter and olive oil. Saute for 20 minutes or until the vegetables are a deep golden brown. Add the shallot and garlic to the skillet. Saute for 3 minutes.

Reduce the heat to low. Sprinkle the cheddar cheese and Parmesan cheese over the vegetables. Stir until the cheeses melt. In a mixing bowl, add the eggs, heavy whipping cream, salt and black pepper. Whisk until combined and pour into the skillet. Do not stir.

Place a lid on the skillet and cook for 5 minutes or until the eggs are nearly set. Preheat the oven to the broiler position. Remove the skillet from the heat and remove the lid from the skillet. Broil for 2 minutes or until the eggs are set. Remove from the oven and cool for 5 minutes before serving.

Italian Frittata

Makes 8 servings

2 medium red potatoes
8 oz. ground Italian sausage
1 green bell pepper, cut into thin strips
1 1/2 cups chopped purple onion
3 garlic cloves, thinly sliced
2 tbs. olive oil
2 tbs. melted unsalted butter
2 tomatoes, peeled and diced
2 tbs. minced fresh parsley
1 tsp. dried basil
1 tsp. dried oregano
1/4 tsp. salt
1/4 tsp. black pepper
8 beaten eggs
3 tbs. water
1/2 cup freshly grated Parmesan cheese

Peel and dice the potatoes. Add the potatoes to a sauce pan over medium heat. Add water to cover the potatoes. Bring to a boil and cook for 7 minutes or until the potatoes are tender. Remove the pan from the heat and drain all the water from the potatoes.

In a 12" oven proof skillet over medium heat, add the Italian sausage. Stir frequently to break the sausage into crumbles as it cooks. Cook for 8 minutes or until the sausage is well browned and no longer pink. Remove the sausage from the skillet and set aside. Drain off any grease in the skillet.

Add the green bell pepper, onion, garlic, olive oil and butter to the skillet. Saute the vegetables for 5 minutes. Add the potatoes, sausage, tomatoes, parsley, basil, oregano, salt and black pepper to the skillet. Stir until combined. Cook for 2 minutes.

In a mixing bowl, add the eggs and water. Whisk until combined and add to the skillet. Stir until combined. Reduce the heat to low. Place a lid on the skillet and cook for 5-8 minutes or until the eggs are set. Remove the skillet from the heat. Sprinkle the Parmesan cheese over the top. Let the frittata sit for 3 minutes before serving.

Italian Garden Frittata

Makes 4 servings

4 eggs
6 egg whites
1/2 cup grated Romano cheese
1 tbs. minced fresh sage
1/2 tsp. salt
1/4 tsp. black pepper
1 tsp. olive oil
1 cup sliced zucchini
2 green onions, sliced
2 plum tomatoes, thinly sliced

In a mixing bowl, add the eggs, egg whites, 1/4 cup Romano cheese, sage, salt and black pepper. Whisk until combined. In a 10" oven proof skillet over medium heat, add the olive oil. When the oil is hot, add the zucchini and green onions. Saute for 4 minutes.

Preheat the oven to the broiler position. Add the eggs to the skillet and reduce the heat to medium low. Place a lid on the skillet. Cook for 4-5 minutes or until the eggs are almost set. Remove the skillet from the heat. Sprinkle 1/4 cup Romano cheese over the frittata. Place the tomato slices over the top.

Broil for 3 minutes or until the eggs are set. Remove from the oven and cool for 5 minutes before serving.

Tomato Topped Frittata

Makes 6 servings

1 tbs. unsalted butter
1 cup frozen cut green beans, thawed
1 cup frozen chunky hashbrowns
1/2 cup chopped red bell pepper
1/2 cup chopped onion
1 garlic clove, minced
8 eggs
1/2 tsp. dried basil
1/2 tsp. salt
1/8 tsp. Tabasco sauce
2 plum tomatoes, sliced
1/2 cup shredded mozzarella cheese

In a 12" skillet over medium heat, add the butter. When the butter melts, add the green beans, hashbrowns, red bell pepper, onion and garlic. Saute for 7 minutes or until the vegetables are crisp tender. Reduce the heat to medium low.

In a mixing bowl, add the eggs, basil, salt and Tabasco sauce. Whisk until combined and pour over the vegetables. Do not stir. When the eggs set around the edges, gently lift the edges with a spatula to allow the uncooked eggs to run underneath.

Place a lid on the skillet. Cook for 10 minutes or until the eggs are set in the center. Place the tomato slices over the top of the frittata. Sprinkle the mozzarella cheese over the tomatoes. Place the lid back on the skillet. Cook for 2 minutes. Remove the skillet from the heat and serve.

Deep Dish Sausage Pizza Frittata

Makes 8 servings

8 oz. ground Italian sausage
3 cups sliced fresh mushrooms
1/4 cup chopped green bell pepper
1/4 cup chopped red onion
12 eggs
1/2 cup marinara sauce
2/3 cup shredded mozzarella cheese
3 tbs. grated Parmesan cheese
2 tbs. minced fresh parsley

Preheat the oven to the broiler position. In a 10" oven proof skillet, add the Italian sausage, mushrooms, green bell pepper and red onion. Stir frequently to break the sausage into crumbles as it cooks. Cook for 8 minutes or until the sausage is well browned and no longer pink. Drain off the excess grease.

In a mixing bowl, add the eggs. Whisk until combined and add to the skillet. Do not stir. Place a lid on the skillet. Cook for 5 minutes or until the eggs are almost set. Remove the skillet from the heat.

Spread the marinara sauce over the top of the eggs. Sprinkle the mozzarella and Parmesan cheese over the top. Broil for 2-3 minutes or until the eggs are set and the cheeses melted. Remove from the oven and sprinkle the parsley over the top.

Fresh Vegetable Gazpacho Frittata

Makes 6 servings

3/4 cup finely chopped fresh tomato
3/4 cup finely chopped zucchini
3/4 cup finely chopped cucumber
8 oz. bottle mild taco sauce
1/4 cup unsalted butter
1 cup chopped onions
12 eggs
2 tbs. water
Salt and black pepper to taste
1 cup shredded cheddar cheese

In a small bowl, add the tomato, zucchini, cucumber and taco sauce. Stir until combined and set aside. In a large skillet, add the butter. When the butter melts, add the onions. Saute for 5 minutes.

In a mixing bowl, add the eggs and water. Season to taste with salt and black pepper. Whisk until combined and add to the skillet. Do not stir. Reduce the heat to low. As the edges of the frittata set, lift the edges with a spatula to allow the uncooked egg to run underneath. Place a lid on the skillet. Cook for 3 minutes or until the top of the frittata is set. Remove the pan from the heat and sprinkle the cheddar cheese over the top.

Place the lid back on the skillet and let the frittata sit for 5 minutes. Cut the frittata into wedges. Spoon the vegetable sauce over the frittata and serve.

Skillet Corn Frittata

Serve for breakfast, lunch or dinner.

Makes 4 servings

3 tbs. unsalted butter
1/4 cup sliced green onion
11 oz. can Mexicorn, drained
6 beaten eggs
1/3 cup whole milk
1/2 tsp. dried oregano
1/8 tsp. black pepper
1 cup sliced fresh tomato
1 cup thinly sliced green bell pepper
1/2 cup shredded Swiss cheese

In a 9" skillet over medium heat, add the butter. When the butter melts, add the green onions. Saute for 3 minutes. Add the corn and stir until combined. In a mixing bowl, add the eggs, milk, oregano and black pepper. Stir until combined and pour into the skillet. Do not stir.

Place a lid on the skillet and reduce the heat to medium low. Cook for 10 minutes or until the frittata is set. The top will still be moist at this point. Place the tomato slices over the frittata. Sprinkle the green bell pepper and Swiss cheese over the tomatoes.

Place the lid back on the skillet. Cook for 5 minutes or until the frittata is set and the cheese melted. Remove the skillet from the heat and serve.

Barley, Bean & Corn Frittata

Makes 6 servings

2 cups water
1/2 cup dry pearl barley
3/4 tsp. salt
2 tsp. olive oil
15 oz. can black beans, rinsed & drained
2 cups shredded cheddar cheese
3/4 cup cooked whole kernel corn
1/2 cup chopped green bell pepper
1/4 cup chopped fresh cilantro
7 eggs
1 cup cottage cheese
1/2 tsp. cayenne pepper
1 cup salsa

Add the water to a sauce pan over medium heat. When the water is boiling, stir in the barley and 1/4 teaspoon salt. Reduce the heat to low and place a lid on the pan. Simmer for 45 minutes or until the barley is tender. Remove the pan from the heat and let the barley sit for 5 minutes. Drain off any remaining water.

Preheat the oven to 400°. Grease a 10" oven proof skillet with the olive oil. Spread the barley in the bottom of the skillet. Spread the black beans over the barley. Sprinkle 1 cup cheddar cheese, corn, green bell pepper and cilantro over the beans.

In a mixing bowl, add the eggs, 1/2 teaspoon salt, cottage cheese and cayenne pepper. Whisk until combined and pour over the beans and barley in the skillet. Do not stir.

Bake for 30 minutes or until the frittata is set in the center. Sprinkle 1 cup cheddar cheese over the top. Bake for 3 minutes or until the cheese melts. Remove from the oven and spread the salsa over the top.

Herb & Vegetable Baked Frittata

Makes 12 servings

1 lb. fresh asparagus, trimmed & cut into 1" pieces
8 oz. sliced fresh mushrooms
1 red bell pepper, diced
1 yellow bell pepper, diced
1 cup chopped onion
3 green onions, chopped
3 tbs. olive oil
2 garlic cloves, minced
3 plum tomatoes, chopped
14 beaten eggs
2 cups shredded Colby Jack cheese
3 tbs. minced fresh parsley
3 tbs. minced fresh basil
1/2 tsp. salt
1/4 tsp. black pepper
1/2 cup shredded Parmesan cheese

Preheat the oven to 350°. In a large skillet over medium heat, add the asparagus, mushrooms, red bell pepper, yellow bell pepper, onion, green onions and olive oil. Saute for 10 minutes or until the vegetables are tender. Add the garlic to the skillet. Saute for 2 minutes. Remove the skillet from the heat and stir in the tomatoes.

In a mixing bowl, add the eggs, Colby Jack cheese, parsley, basil, salt and black pepper. Whisk until combined and add the vegetables to the bowl. Stir until combined. Spray a 9 x 13 baking pan with non stick cooking spray. Spoon the frittata into the pan.

Bake for 40 minutes. Sprinkle the Parmesan cheese over the top. Bake for 12-15 minutes or until a knife inserted in the center of the frittata comes out clean. Remove from the oven and cool for 5 minutes before serving.

Potato Mushroom Frittata

Makes 4 servings

5 eggs, at room temperature
2 egg whites, at room temperature
1 cup diced new potatoes
1/2 cup sliced fresh mushrooms
2 tbs. sliced green onions
1 garlic clove, minced
4 tsp. chopped fresh basil
1/2 cup chopped fresh tomato
2 tbs. grated Parmesan cheese

In a mixing bowl, add the eggs and egg whites. Whisk until well combined. Spray a 10" skillet with non stick cooking spray. Place the skillet over medium heat. When the skillet is hot, add the potatoes. Stir occasionally and place a lid on the skillet. Cook about 5 minutes or until the potatoes begin brown and are almost tender.

Add the mushrooms, green onions, garlic and 2 teaspoons basil to the skillet. Saute for 5 minutes or until the potatoes and vegetables are tender. Pour the eggs in the skillet. Do not stir. When the eggs set around the edges, gently lift the edges with a spatula to allow the uncooked eggs to run underneath.

Place a lid on the skillet. Cook for 3-5 minutes or until the eggs are set in the center. Sprinkle the tomato and Parmesan cheese over the top. Place the lid on the skillet and cook for 2 minutes. Remove the skillet from the heat and sprinkle 2 teaspoons basil over the top.

Vegetable Frittata Pie

Makes 6 servings

9" refrigerated pie crust
2 tsp. vegetable oil
2 pkgs. frozen broccoli & cauliflower, 10 oz. size
1 cup chopped onion
2 garlic cloves, minced
4 beaten eggs
1/4 tsp. black pepper
1/3 cup grated Parmesan cheese
1 tsp. dried basil
1/2 tsp. salt

Preheat the oven to 400°. Place the pie crust in a 9" pie pan. Trim and flute the edges as desired. In a skillet over medium heat, add the vegetable oil. When the oil is hot, add the broccoli & cauliflower, onion and garlic. Saute for 7 minutes or until the vegetables are partially thawed. Remove the skillet from the heat.

In a mixing bowl, add the eggs, black pepper, Parmesan cheese, basil and salt. Stir until well combined. Add the vegetables to the pie crust. Pour the eggs over the top. Do not stir. Bake for 30 minutes or until the vegetables are tender and the pie set in the center. Remove from the oven and cool for 5 minutes before serving.

Note: I have baked this many times without the crust. Prepare as directed above omitting the crust. Spray the pie pan with non stick cooking spray if omitting the crust.

Eggplant & Roasted Pepper Frittata

Makes 6 servings

2 cups peeled & chopped eggplant
3 tbs. olive oil
12 oz. jar roasted red bell peppers, drained & chopped
10 eggs
1/2 cup whole milk
1 tsp. salt
1/4 tsp. black pepper
1/4 cup freshly grated Parmesan cheese

In a 10" oven proof skillet over medium heat, add the eggplant and olive oil. Saute for 4 minutes or until the eggplant is tender. Add the roasted red bell peppers to the skillet. Saute for 1 minute.

In a mixing bowl, add the eggs, milk, salt and black pepper. Whisk until combined and add to the skillet. Do not stir. As the edges of the eggs set, lift the edges of the frittata with a spatula to let the uncooked eggs run underneath.

Place a lid on the skillet and reduce the heat to low. Cook for 8 minutes or until the center of the frittata is set. Remove the skillet from the heat. Sprinkle the Parmesan cheese over the top of the frittata. Turn the oven to the broiler position. Broil for 2 minutes or until the edges of the frittata are golden brown. Remove from the oven and serve.

Tomato Herb Mini Frittatas

Makes 8 servings

12 eggs
1 cup half and half
1/2 tsp. salt
1/4 tsp. black pepper
2 tbs. chopped fresh chives
1 tbs. chopped fresh parsley
1 tsp. chopped fresh oregano
1 pint grape tomatoes, halved
1 1/2 cups shredded Italian cheese blend

Preheat the oven to 450°. Spray eight 6 oz. custard cups with non stick cooking spray. Add the eggs, half and half, salt and black pepper to a blender. Process until well combined. In a small bowl, add the chives, parsley and oregano. Stir until combined.

Place the custard cups on 2 large baking sheets. Place the tomatoes, chive blend and 1 cup Italian cheese blend in the custard cups. Stir until combined. Pour the eggs into the custard cups. Do not stir. Sprinkle 1/2 cup Italian cheese blend over the eggs.

Bake for 12-15 minutes or until a toothpick inserted in the center of the frittatas comes out clean. Remove the baking sheets from the oven and serve.

Everyday Frittata

This frittata is great for breakfast, brunch or dinner.

Makes 4 servings

8 eggs
1/2 tsp. dried oregano
1/8 tsp. black pepper
1 cup chopped onion
1 garlic clove, minced
1 tsp. unsalted butter
3 plum tomatoes, chopped
1/2 cup crumbled feta cheese
2 tbs. capers, drained

In a mixing bowl, add the eggs, oregano and black pepper. Whisk until combined. In a 10" oven proof skillet, add the onion, garlic and butter. Place the skillet over medium heat and saute for 3 minutes. Add the tomatoes to the skillet. Saute for 1 minute.

Add the eggs to the skillet. Do not stir. Reduce the heat to low and place a lid on the skillet. Cook for 4 minutes or until the eggs are almost set. Remove the skillet from the heat.

Preheat the oven to the broiler position. Sprinkle the feta cheese and capers over the top of the frittata. Broil for 2 minutes or until the eggs are set. Remove from the oven and cool for 5 minutes before serving.

Zucchini Onion Frittata

Makes 6 servings

3 tbs. unsalted butter
2 tbs. vegetable oil
2 medium zucchini, thinly sliced
1 onion, cut in half and sliced
1/2 cup grated Parmesan cheese
8 eggs
1/4 cup whole milk
1 tsp. salt
1/2 tsp. black pepper
1/4 cup chopped fresh basil
1 cup diced fresh tomato

Add the butter and vegetable oil to a 12" oven proof skillet over medium heat. When the butter melts, add the zucchini and onion. Saute for 12 minutes or until the onion is golden brown. Remove the skillet from the heat and stir in 1/4 cup Parmesan cheese.

In a mixing bowl, add the eggs, milk, salt and black pepper. Whisk until combined and add to the skillet. Do not stir. Preheat the oven to 350°. Bake for 15 minutes or until the frittata is set in the center. Turn the oven to the broiler position. Sprinkle 1/4 cup Parmesan cheese over the top. Broil for 2 minutes or until the edges of the frittata are lightly browned. Remove the skillet from the oven and sprinkle the basil and tomatoes over the top. Serve immediately.

Zucchini Swiss Frittata

Makes 2 servings

1/2 cup chopped onion
1 cup shredded zucchini
1 tsp. olive oil
3 eggs
1/4 tsp. salt
1 cup shredded Swiss cheese

Add the onion, zucchini and olive oil to an 8" oven proof skillet over medium heat. Saute for 5 minutes. In a mixing bowl, add the eggs and salt. Whisk until combined and pour over the the vegetables in the skillet. Do not stir and cook for 5-6 minutes or until the eggs are almost set. Sprinkle the Swiss cheese over the top.

Preheat the oven to 350°. Remove the skillet from the heat and place in the oven. Bake for 5 minutes or until the eggs are set and the cheese bubbly. Remove from the oven and serve.

Garlic Frittata

Makes 4 servings

1 tbs. unsalted butter
1 tbs. finely chopped onion
4 garlic cloves, minced
1 zucchini, shredded & patted dry
6 eggs
1/4 tsp. ground mustard
4 bacon slices, cooked & crumbled
1/4 tsp. salt
1/8 tsp. black pepper
1/4 cup shredded Swiss cheese
1/4 cup sliced green onions

Add the butter to a 10" oven proof skillet over medium heat. When the butter melts, add the onion and garlic. Saute for 1 minute. Add the zucchini to the skillet. Saute 3 minutes.

In a mixing bowl, add the eggs and ground mustard. Whisk until combined and pour into the skillet. Do not stir. Sprinkle the bacon, salt and black pepper over the omelet. As the eggs set around the edges, gently lift the edges to allow the uncooked eggs to run underneath. Cook about 6 minutes or until the eggs are almost set. Remove from the heat.

Preheat the oven to the broiler position. Broil for 1 minute or until the eggs are completely set. Remove from the oven and sprinkle the Swiss cheese and green onions over the top. Let the frittata sit for 2 minutes before serving.

Veggie Frittata

Makes 8 servings

1 onion, chopped
1 1/2 cups sliced fresh mushrooms
1 tbs. olive oil
6 oz. pkg. fresh baby spinach
4 eggs
6 egg whites
1 cup shredded sharp cheddar cheese
1/4 cup grated Parmesan cheese
2 tbs. whole milk
1/2 tsp. black pepper
1/4 tsp. salt
1/4 tsp. ground nutmeg

In a 10" oven proof skillet over medium heat, add the onion, mushrooms and olive oil. Saute for 10 minutes. Add the spinach and saute for 3 minutes. Remove the skillet from the heat and drain off any liquid.

Preheat the oven to 350°. In a mixing bowl, add the eggs, egg whites, cheddar cheese, Parmesan cheese, milk, black pepper, salt and nutmeg. Whisk until combined and add to the skillet. Stir until combined.

Bake for 15 minutes or until the center of the frittata is set. Remove the skillet from the oven and cool for 5 minutes before serving.

Spinach Tomato Frittata

Makes 4 servings

6 eggs
1/3 cup grated Parmesan cheese
1/2 tsp. garlic powder
1/2 tsp. dried basil
1/4 tsp. salt
1/4 tsp. black pepper
1/8 tsp. ground nutmeg
2 tsp. olive oil
6 cups fresh spinach
6 cherry tomatoes, quartered

In a small bowl, add the eggs, Parmesan cheese, garlic powder, basil, salt, black pepper and nutmeg. Whisk until well combined. In a skillet over medium heat, add the olive oil. When the oil is hot, add the spinach. Saute for 3 minutes.

Reduce the heat to low. Spread the spinach evenly in the skillet. Sprinkle the tomatoes over the spinach. Pour the eggs over the spinach but do not stir. Place a lid on the skillet. When the bottom of the frittata is set, lift the edges to allow the uncooked eggs to run underneath. Cook for 12 minutes or until the frittata is set in the center and the bottom browned. Remove the skillet from the heat and serve.

Asparagus Frittata

Makes 6 servings

1 lb. fresh asparagus
2 tbs. unsalted butter
1/2 cup chopped onion
1 garlic clove, minced
12 eggs
1/2 cup sour cream
3/4 tsp. black pepper
1/2 tsp. salt
1 cup shredded Gouda cheese
1/4 cup shredded Parmesan cheese

Preheat the oven to 350°. Trim the woody ends from the asparagus and cut the asparagus into 1" pieces. In a 10" skillet over medium heat, add the asparagus, butter, onion and garlic. Saute the vegetables for 5 minutes or until they are tender.

In a mixing bowl, add the eggs, sour cream, black pepper, salt and 3/4 cup Gouda cheese. Whisk until combined and pour over the vegetables in the skillet. Do not stir and cook for 3 minutes. Remove the skillet from the heat and place the skillet in the oven.

Bake for 5 minutes. Sprinkle 1/4 cup Gouda cheese and the Parmesan cheese over the top of the frittata. Bake for 5 minutes or until the frittata is set in the center and golden brown. Remove the skillet from the oven and serve.

Spring Frittata

Makes 4 servings

4 tsp. olive oil
8 oz. trimmed fresh asparagus, cut into 1" pieces
1 red bell pepper, thinly sliced
8 beaten eggs
1 tbs. finely chopped fresh basil
1/4 tsp. salt

In a 10" skillet over medium heat, add 2 teaspoons olive oil. When the oil is hot, add the asparagus and red bell pepper. Saute for 5 minutes. Remove the skillet from the heat and add the vegetables to a mixing bowl. Add the eggs, basil and salt to the bowl. Whisk until combined.

Add 2 teaspoons olive oil to the skillet. Place the skillet back on the heat. Add the eggs to the skillet. When the eggs are set on the bottom, lift the edges of the frittata to allow the uncooked eggs to flow underneath. Cook for 5 minutes or until the top of the frittata is set and the bottom golden brown. Remove the skillet from the heat and invert the skillet onto a serving platter. Cut into wedges and serve.

Feta Asparagus Frittata

Makes 2 servings

12 fresh asparagus spears, trimmed
2 tbs. water
2 green onions, chopped
1 garlic clove, minced
1 tbs. olive oil
6 eggs
2 tbs. heavy whipping cream
1/8 tsp. salt
1/8 tsp. black pepper
1/2 cup crumbled feta cheese

In an 8" oven proof skillet over medium heat, add the asparagus and water. Cook for 4 minutes or until the water evaporates and the asparagus are crisp tender. Remove the asparagus from the skillet. Chop 2 asparagus spears.

Add the green onions, garlic and olive oil to the skillet. Saute for 4 minutes. In a mixing bowl, add the eggs, 2 chopped asparagus spears, heavy whipping cream, salt and black pepper. Whisk until combined and add to the skillet. Do not stir. Place a lid on the skillet and cook for 4 minutes or until the eggs are almost set. Remove the skillet from the heat.

Preheat the oven to 350°. Place the 10 remaining asparagus spears over the top of the eggs. Sprinkle the feta cheese over the top. Bake for 7 minutes or until the eggs are set. Remove from the oven and serve.

Tomato Asparagus Frittata

Makes 6 servings

4 oz. fresh asparagus, trimmed & cut in half
1 cup sliced fresh mushrooms
1/3 cup chopped onion
1/4 cup unsalted butter
6 beaten eggs
8 bacon slices, cooked & crumbled
1 tomato, sliced
1 cup shredded cheddar cheese

In a 9" skillet over medium heat, add the asparagus, mushrooms, onion and butter. Saute for 5 minutes or until the vegetables are tender. Reduce the heat to medium low. Pour the eggs over the vegetables in the skillet. Do not stir. Sprinkle the bacon over the top.

As the edges of the frittata set, gently lift the edges so the uncooked eggs runs underneath. Cook for 5 minutes or until the eggs are set. Place the tomatoes over the top. Sprinkle the cheddar cheese over the tomatoes. Remove the skillet from the heat and serve.

Sweet Potato Frittata

Makes 2 servings

1 large sweet potato, peeled & diced
1 shallot, minced
1 garlic clove, minced
2 tbs. olive oil
Salt and black pepper to taste
4 beaten eggs
1 cup half and half
1/2 cup grated Parmesan cheese
1/4 cup chopped fresh sage leaves, optional

Preheat the oven to 400°. Spray an 8" baking dish with non stick cooking spray. Add the sweet potatoes, shallot, garlic and olive oil to the baking dish. Stir until combined. Season to taste with salt and black pepper.

Bake for 25 minutes or until the sweet potatoes are tender. In a mixing bowl, add the eggs, half and half and Parmesan cheese. Whisk until combined and stir into the sweet potatoes. Sprinkle the sage leaves over the top. Bake for 15 minutes or until the eggs are set. Remove from the oven and cool for 5 minutes before serving.

New Potato Frittata

Makes 6 servings

8 oz. small red new potatoes, washed
1 1/2 tsp. salt
3 tbs. olive oil
1 cup chopped onion
1/4 cup chopped parsley
8 eggs
3 tbs. fresh breadcrumbs
3 tbs. grated Parmesan cheese
2 tsp. all purpose flour
2 tbs. half and half
1/4 tsp. black pepper

Add the potatoes to a sauce pan over medium heat. Sprinkle 1 teaspoon salt over the potatoes. Add water to cover the potatoes. Bring to a boil and cook for 12-15 minutes or until the potatoes are almost tender. Remove the pan from the heat and drain all the water from the pan. Cool for 15 minutes.

In a 10" oven proof skillet, add 2 tablespoons olive oil. When the oil is hot, add the onion. Saute for 5 minutes. Remove the pan from the heat and stir in the parsley. Cool for 10 minutes.

In a separate mixing bowl, add the eggs, breadcrumbs, Parmesan cheese, all purpose flour, half and half, 1/2 teaspoon salt and black pepper. Whisk until combined. Chop the potatoes and add to the bowl. Add the onions and parsley to the bowl. Stir until combined.

Preheat the oven to the broiler position. Add 1 tablespoon olive oil to the skillet and place over medium heat. When the oil is warm, add the eggs to the skillet. When the eggs are set on the bottom, gently lift the sides with a spatula to allow the uncooked eggs to run underneath. Remove the skillet from the heat. Place in the oven and cook for 1-2 minutes or until the eggs are set and the frittata begins to brown. Remove from the oven and serve.

Potato & Bacon Frittata

Makes 8 servings

10 eggs
1/4 cup minced fresh parsley
3 tbs. whole milk
1/4 tsp. salt
1/8 tsp. black pepper
8 bacon slices, chopped
2 medium potatoes, peeled & thinly sliced
2 green onions, finely chopped
4 fresh sage leaves, thinly sliced
1 cup shredded pepper jack cheese
2 plum tomatoes, sliced

Preheat the oven to 400°. In a large mixing bowl, add the eggs, parsley, milk, salt and black pepper. Whisk until combined. In a 10" oven proof skillet over medium heat, add the bacon. Cook about 5 minutes or until the bacon is done but not crisp.

Add the potatoes, green onions and sage leaves to the skillet. Stir frequently and cook about 8 minutes or until the potatoes are tender. Remove the skillet from the heat and sprinkle the pepper jack cheese over the top.

Pour the eggs evenly over the vegetables in the skillet. Do not stir. Place the tomato slices over the top. Bake for 20 minutes or until the eggs are completely set. Remove from the oven and let the frittata sit for 10 minutes before serving.

Bacon Tomato Frittata

Makes 4 servings

6 bacon slices
7 eggs
1/4 cup whole milk
1 tsp. Dijon mustard
1 cup chopped fresh tomato
1 garlic clove, minced
1 cup shredded cheddar cheese

In a skillet over medium heat, add the bacon. Cook for 7 minutes or until the bacon is crispy. Remove the bacon from the skillet and drain on paper towels. Crumble the bacon. Drain off all but 1 tablespoon bacon drippings.

In a mixing bowl, add the eggs, milk and Dijon mustard. Whisk until combined. Reduce the heat to low. Add the tomato and garlic to the skillet. Saute for 2 minutes. Add the eggs to the skillet. Do not stir. Sprinkle the bacon over the eggs.

As the edges of the eggs cook, gently lift the edges to allow the uncooked eggs to run underneath. Place a lid on the skillet. Cook for 4-5 minutes or until the frittata is completely set. Remove the skillet from the heat and sprinkle the cheddar cheese over the top. Let the cheese sit for 3 minutes before serving.

Spinach Hashbrown Frittata

Makes 8 servings

1 1/2 cups finely chopped onion
1 tbs. olive oil
2 garlic cloves, minced
10 oz. pkg. frozen spinach, thawed & squeezed dry
1/4 tsp. salt
1/4 tsp. black pepper
2 oz. pancetta, finely chopped
3 cups frozen shredded hashbrowns, thawed
8 beaten eggs
1 cup whole milk
1 cup fontina cheese
1 cup shredded cheddar cheese
2 tbs. minced fresh parsley
1 tbs. Worcestershire sauce
1 tsp. ground mustard
1/8 tsp. ground nutmeg

Preheat the oven to 350°. In a large skillet over medium heat, add the onions and olive oil. Saute for 6 minutes. Add the garlic and saute for 1 minute. Add the spinach, salt and black pepper to the skillet. Stir until combined and cook only until the spinach is heated. Remove the skillet from the heat.

In a small skillet over medium heat, add the pancetta. Cook about 4 minutes or until the pancetta is crispy. Remove the skillet from the heat and drain the pancetta on paper towels. Spray a 11 x 7 casserole dish with non stick cooking spray.

Place the hashbrowns in the bottom of the casserole dish. Spoon the spinach filling over the hashbrowns. Sprinkle the pancetta over the top. In a mixing bowl, add the eggs, milk, 1/2 cup fontina cheese, 1/2 cup cheddar cheese, parsley, Worcestershire sauce, ground mustard and nutmeg. Whisk until combined and pour over the top of the dish. Do not stir. Sprinkle 1/2 cup fontina cheese and 1/2 cup cheddar cheese over the top.

Bake for 35-40 minutes or until a knife inserted near the center of the frittata comes out clean. Remove from the oven and let the frittata sit for 10 minutes before cutting.

Fajita Frittata

Makes 8 servings

8 oz. boneless skinless chicken breast, cut into thin strips
1 cup onion, cut into thin strips
1/2 cup green bell pepper, cut into thin strips
1 tsp. lime juice
1/2 tsp. salt
1/2 tsp. ground cumin
1/2 tsp. chili powder
2 tbs. vegetable oil
8 beaten eggs
1 cup shredded Colby Jack cheese

In a skillet over medium heat, add the chicken, onion, green bell pepper, lime juice, salt, cumin, chili powder and vegetable oil. Saute for 5 minutes or until the chicken is no longer pink.

Pour the eggs over the chicken. Do not stir. Place a lid on the skillet. Cook for 8 minutes or until the eggs are almost set. Remove from the heat. Preheat the oven to the broiler position. Remove the lid from the skillet. Broil for 2-3 minutes or until the eggs are completely set. Remove from the oven and sprinkle the Colby Jack cheese over the top of the eggs. Place the lid back on the skillet and let sit for 3 minutes before serving.

Basic Omelet

Fill the omelet with your favorite fillings.

Makes 1 serving

2 eggs
1/8 tsp. salt
1/8 tsp. white pepper
1 tbs. water
1 tbs. unsalted butter

In a small bowl, add the eggs, salt, white pepper and water. Stir until well combined. Place an 8" skillet over medium heat. When the skillet is hot, add the butter. When the butter melts, add the eggs.

As the edges of the eggs set, lift the edges of the omelet with a spatula to let the uncooked eggs run underneath. When the center of the omelet is almost set, sprinkle your filling toppings over the omelet. Using a spatula, fold the omelet over the filling. Place a lid on the skillet and cook for 1 minute or until the omelet is set and the filling ingredients hot. Remove the skillet from the heat and serve.

Baked Omelets

Makes 3 omelets

2 beaten eggs
1/2 cup all purpose flour
1/4 tsp. salt
1 cup whole milk
3 tbs. unsalted butter

Preheat the oven to 450°. In a mixing bowl, add the eggs, all purpose flour, salt and milk. Whisk until well combined. Add 1 tablespoon butter to three 9" round cake pans. Place the pans in the oven until the butter melts. Remove the pans from the oven.

Spoon 1/3 of the egg mixture into each pan. Bake for 7 minutes. Reduce the heat to 350°. Bake for 5 minutes or until the omelets are browned. The omelets will puff up while baking. Remove the omelets from the oven. It is normal for the omelets to settle when removed from the oven. Serve immediately.

Monterey Jack Baked Omelet

Makes 6 servings

8 bacon slices, diced
4 green onions, diced
8 eggs
1 cup whole milk
1/2 tsp. season salt
2 1/2 cups shredded Monterey Jack cheese

Preheat the oven to 350°. In a skillet over medium heat, add the bacon. Cook for 6 minutes or until the bacon is crisp. Remove the bacon from the skillet and drain on paper towels. Drain off all but 1 tablespoon bacon drippings. Add the green onions to the skillet. Saute for 3 minutes. Remove the skillet from the heat.

In a mixing bowl, add the eggs. Whisk until combined. Add the milk, season salt, 2 cups Monterey Jack cheese, bacon and green onions. Stir until combined. Spray a 2 quart casserole dish with non stick cooking spray. Spoon the omelet into the casserole dish.

Bake for 35-40 minutes or until the omelet is set. Sprinkle 1/2 cup Monterey Jack cheese over the top. Bake for 3 minutes or until the cheese melts. Remove from the oven and serve.

Spanish Omelet

Makes 4 servings

1/2 cup chopped green bell pepper
1/2 cup sliced fresh mushrooms
4 tbs. melted unsalted butter
3/4 cup diced plum tomato
6 eggs
1/4 cup water
1/2 tsp. salt
1/8 tsp. black pepper
4 bacon slices, cooked and crumbled
1/2 cup picante sauce

In a skillet over medium heat, add the green bell pepper, mushrooms and 2 tablespoons butter. Saute for 5 minutes. Add the tomato and cook for 1 minute. Remove the vegetables from the skillet and set aside. Drain off any liquid in the skillet.

In a mixing bowl, add the eggs, water, salt and black pepper. Whisk until combined. Place the skillet back on the stove. Add 1 tablespoon butter to the skillet. When the butter melts, add half the eggs. As the edges of the eggs set, lift the edges of the omelet with a spatula to let the uncooked eggs run underneath.

When the center of the omelet is almost set, spoon half the vegetables and bacon over the omelet. Using a spatula, fold the omelet over the filling. Place a lid on the skillet and cook for 1 minute or until the omelet is set and the filling ingredients hot. Remove the omelet from the skillet and keep warm while you prepare the remaining omelet. Repeat the steps above to make the second omelet. Remove the skillet from the heat and spoon the picante sauce over the top.

Refried Bean Omelet

Makes 2 servings

6 eggs
1/4 cup water
1 cup warm refried beans
1/4 cup chopped onion
1/2 cup shredded Mexican cheese blend
1/4 cup salsa

Spray a 10" oven proof skillet with non stick cooking spray. In a mixing bowl, add the eggs and water. Whisk until combined. Place the skillet over medium heat. When the skillet is hot, add half the eggs. As the eggs set, lift the edges with a spatula to allow the uncooked eggs to run underneath. Cook for 2-3 minutes or until the eggs are set.

Spread 1/2 cup refried beans over one side of the omelet. Sprinkle 1/8 cup chopped onion and 1/8 cup Mexican cheese blend over the beans. Fold the omelet over the filling. Slide the omelet onto a serving plate. Repeat the steps making the second omelet. Spoon 1/8 cup salsa over each omelet. Sprinkle the remaining Mexican cheese blend over the top and serve.

Chorizo Salsa Omelet

Makes 1 serving

1 tbs. unsalted butter
3 eggs
3 tbs. water
1/8 tsp. salt
1/8 tsp. black pepper
1/4 cup cooked chorizo sausage
2 tbs. salsa

In a small skillet over medium heat, add the butter. In a small bowl, add the eggs, water, salt and black pepper. Whisk until combined. When the butter melts, add the eggs. Do not stir. As the eggs set, lift the edges of the omelet to allow the uncooked eggs to run underneath. Cook for 3-4 minutes or until the omelet is set.

When the eggs are set, spoon the chorizo and salsa on one side of the omelet. Fold the other side over the filling. Remove from the heat and serve.

Mexican Omelet Roll Ups With Avocado Sauce

Makes 8 servings

8 eggs, beaten
2 tbs. whole milk
Salt and black pepper to taste
1 tbs. unsalted butter
1 1/2 cups shredded Monterey Jack cheese
1 1/2 cups diced fresh tomato
1/4 cup chopped fresh cilantro
8 corn tortillas
1 1/2 cups salsa
2 avocados, peeled, pitted & chopped
1/4 cup sour cream
2 tbs. finely chopped onion
1 jalapeno pepper, seeded & minced
1 tsp. lime juice
1/4 tsp. salt
1/4 tsp. minced garlic

Preheat the oven to 350°. Spray a 9 x 13 baking pan with non stick cooking spray. In a mixing bowl, add the eggs and milk. Whisk until combined and season to taste with salt and black pepper.

Add the butter to a skillet over medium heat. When the butter melts, add the eggs. Stir frequently and cook until the eggs are set. Add the Monterey Jack cheese, tomato and cilantro to the skillet. Stir until combined and remove the skillet from the heat.

Spoon the egg filling in the center of the corn tortillas. Roll the tortillas up. Place the tortillas, seam side down, in the baking pan. Pour the salsa over the tortillas. Cover the pan with aluminum foil. Bake for 20 minutes. Remove from the oven.

Add the avocados, sour cream, onion, jalapeno pepper, lime juice, 1/4 teaspoon salt and garlic to a blender. Process until smooth and combined. Serve the sauce with the tortillas.

Mediterranean Broccoli Cheese Omelet

Makes 4 servings

2 1/2 cups fresh broccoli florets
3 tbs. water
6 eggs
1/4 cup whole milk
1/2 tsp. salt
1/4 tsp. black pepper
1/3 cup grated Romano cheese
1/3 cup pitted sliced kalamata olives
1 tbs. olive oil
1 tbs. minced fresh parsley
2 tbs. shaved Parmesan cheese

Add the broccoli florets and water to a microwavable bowl. Microwave for 6 minutes or until the broccoli is tender. Remove from the microwave and drain off any water.

In a mixing bowl, add the eggs, milk, salt and black pepper. Whisk until combined and stir in the broccoli, Romano cheese and olives. In a 10" oven proof skillet over medium heat, add the olive oil. When the oil is hot, add the eggs. Do not stir. Cook for 4 minutes or until the eggs are almost set. Remove the skillet from the heat.

Preheat the oven to the broiler position. Broil for 3 minutes or until the eggs are set. Remove from the oven and sprinkle the parsley and Parmesan cheese over the top. Let the omelet sit for 5 minutes before serving.

Three Pepper Omelet

This is great for most any meal. Add different vegetable fillings to the omelet instead of the peppers for endless variations. Sprinkle shredded cheese over the omelet if desired.

Makes 2 servings

1/3 cup thinly sliced green bell pepper
1/3 cup thinly sliced red bell pepper
1/3 cup thinly sliced yellow bell pepper
1/3 cup chopped onion
2 tsp. chopped fresh basil
4 eggs
2 tbs. whole milk
1/4 tsp. salt
1/8 tsp. black pepper

Spray a 10" skillet with non stick cooking spray. Place the skillet over medium heat. Add the peppers, onion and basil to the skillet. Saute for 3 minutes or until the vegetables are crisp tender. Remove the skillet from the heat and add the peppers to a small bowl.

Wipe the skillet clean with a paper towel. In a mixing bowl, add the eggs, milk, salt and black pepper. Whisk until combined. Spray the skillet with non stick cooking spray and place the skillet over medium heat. Pour the eggs into the skillet. Do not stir.

Cook for 3-4 minutes or until the eggs are set. As the eggs set, lift the edges of the omelet with a spatula to allow the uncooked eggs to run underneath. When the omelet is set, spoon the vegetables over one side of the omelet. Fold the other side over the filling. Remove the skillet from the heat and serve.

Florentine Mushroom Omelet

This also makes an excellent dinner omelet. If serving for dinner, serve with garlic bread and fruit.

Makes 4 servings

10 oz. pkg. frozen chopped spinach, thawed & drained
1 cup sliced fresh mushrooms
1/2 tsp. salt
1/4 tsp. black pepper
8 eggs
1/2 cup shredded Swiss cheese

Spray a 10" skillet with non stick cooking spray. Place the skillet over medium heat and add the spinach, mushrooms, 1/4 teaspoon salt and 1/8 teaspoon black pepper. Saute for 4 minutes. Remove the spinach and mushrooms from the skillet and spoon into a small bowl. Wipe the skillet clean with paper towels.

Spray the skillet with non stick cooking spray and place back on the stove. In a mixing bowl, add the eggs, 1/4 teaspoon salt and 1/8 teaspoon black pepper. Whisk until combined and add to the hot skillet. Do not stir.

Cook for 3-4 minutes or until the eggs are set. As the eggs set, lift the edges of the omelet with a spatula to allow the uncooked eggs to run underneath. When the omelet is set, spoon the spinach and mushrooms over one side of the omelet. Sprinkle the Swiss cheese over the top of the filling. Fold the other side over the filling. Remove the skillet from the heat and serve.

Baked Vegetable Omelet

Makes 12 servings

12 eggs
1/3 cup whole milk
1/4 cup melted unsalted butter
1/2 tsp. salt
1/4 tsp. black pepper
1/4 tsp. ground nutmeg
16 oz. pkg. frozen broccoli, cauliflower & carrots, thawed
1 1/2 cups shredded Swiss cheese
1/3 cup chopped green onions

Preheat the oven to 350°. Spray a 9 x 13 baking pan with non stick cooking spray. In a mixing bowl, add the eggs, milk, butter, salt, black pepper and nutmeg. Whisk until combined. Add the thawed vegetables and 1 cup Swiss cheese to the bowl. Whisk until combined and pour into the baking pan.

Bake for 25 minutes or until the omelet is completely set and the vegetables tender. Remove from the oven and sprinkle 1/2 cup Swiss cheese and the green onions over the top. Let the omelet sit for 3 minutes before serving.

Cream Cheese & Chive Omelet

Makes 2 servings

1 tbs. olive oil
4 eggs
2 tbs. minced fresh chives
2 tbs. water
1/8 tsp. salt
1/8 tsp. black pepper
2 oz. cream cheese, cubed
2 tbs. salsa

Add the olive oil to a skillet over medium heat. In a mixing bowl, add the eggs, chives, water, salt and black pepper. Whisk until combined. When the oil is hot, add the eggs. Do not stir. When the eggs are set on the bottom and edges, lift the edges with a spatula to allow the uncooked eggs to run underneath.

Cook about 3 minutes or until the eggs are set. Sprinkle the cream cheese on one side of the omelet. Fold the omelet over the cream cheese. Remove from the heat and place on a serving plate. Spoon the salsa over the top and serve.

Monterey Jack Omelets With Bacon Avocado Salsa

Makes 2 servings

6 cooked bacon slices, crumbled
1 cup shredded Monterey Jack cheese
1 avocado, peeled and diced
1/4 cup salsa
1/4 cup minced fresh cilantro
6 eggs
2 tbs. water
1/2 tsp. salt
1/4 tsp. black pepper
1/4 cup unsalted butter

In a small bowl, add the bacon, 1/2 cup Monterey Jack cheese, avocado and salsa. Stir until combined. In a separate small bowl, add 1/2 cup Monterey Jack cheese and cilantro. Stir until combined.

In a mixing bowl, add the eggs, water, salt and black pepper. Whisk until well combined. In a 9" non stick skillet, add 2 tablespoons butter. Place the skillet over medium heat. When the butter melts, add half the eggs. Sprinkle half the cilantro cheese mixture over the eggs.

As the eggs cook on the bottom, gently lift the edges of the eggs to allow the uncooked eggs to run underneath. Cook for 1 minute or until the eggs are set. Sprinkle half of the bacon filling over one side of the omelet. Fold the remaining half of the omelet over the filling. Let the omelet cook for 45 seconds. Remove the omelet from the skillet and place on a platter. Repeat the steps using the remaining eggs, bacon filling and cilantro cheese mixture.

Baked Rolled Vegetable Omelet

You can substitute 2 cups of your favorite omelet filling for the vegetables if desired. Omit the Italian seasoning if not using the vegetables or season with salt and black pepper.

Makes 8 servings

4 oz. cream cheese, softened
3/4 cup whole milk
1/4 cup plus 2 tbs. grated Parmesan cheese
2 tbs. all purpose flour
12 eggs
1 cup chopped green bell pepper
1 cup sliced fresh mushrooms
1/2 cup chopped onion
2 tsp. vegetable oil
1 1/2 cups shredded mozzarella cheese
1 plum tomato, chopped
1 1/4 tsp. dried Italian seasoning

Preheat the oven to 375°. Spray a 15 x 10 x 1 baking pan with non stick cooking spray. Line the bottom of the pan with parchment paper. Spray the parchment paper with non stick cooking spray.

In a mixing bowl, add the cream cheese and milk. Whisk until smooth and combined. Add 1/4 cup Parmesan cheese and the all purpose flour to the bowl. Whisk until combined.

In a separate bowl, add the eggs. Whisk until combined and add the cream cheese mixture to the eggs. Whisk until smooth and combined. Pour the eggs in the baking pan. Bake for 20 minutes or until the eggs are set in the center. Remove the pan from the oven.

While the eggs cook, make the filling. In a skillet over medium heat, add the green bell pepper, mushrooms, onions and vegetable oil. Saute for 6 minutes or until the vegetables are tender. Remove from the heat and keep the vegetables warm while the eggs bake.

Invert the omelet in the baking pan onto your work surface. Sprinkle the vegetables, mozzarella cheese, tomato and 1 teaspoon Italian seasoning over the omelet. Starting with a short side, roll the omelet up and place on a serving platter. Sprinkle 2 tablespoons Parmesan cheese and 1/2 teaspoon Italian seasoning over the top. Using a serrated knife, cut into slices and serve.

Asparagus Crab Omelets

Makes 4 servings

8 eggs
2 tbs. whole milk
Salt and black pepper to taste
1 1/2 tsp. vegetable oil
2 cups shredded cheddar cheese
2 cups chopped fresh asparagus, cooked
2 cups cooked crabmeat, chopped
1 cup warm hollandaise sauce
1 tsp. minced fresh chives

In a mixing bowl, add the eggs and milk. Season to taste with salt and black pepper. Whisk until well combined. In a 10" skillet over medium heat, add 3/4 teaspoon vegetable oil. When the oil is hot, add half the eggs.

As the edges of the eggs set, lift the edges of the omelet with a spatula to let the uncooked eggs run underneath. When the center of the omelet is almost set, sprinkle 1/2 cup cheddar cheese over the omelet. Sprinkle 1 cup asparagus and 1 cup crabmeat over the omelet. Sprinkle 1/2 cup cheddar cheese over the crab. Using a spatula, fold the omelet over the filling. Place a lid on the skillet and cook for 2 minutes or until the omelet is set. Remove the skillet from the heat and place the omelet on a serving plate. Repeat the steps using the remaining eggs, cheddar cheese, vegetable oil, asparagus and crab.

Spoon the hollandaise sauce over the omelets. Sprinkle the chives over the top and serve.

Italian Pizza Omelet

Makes 1 serving

3/4 cup sliced fresh mushrooms
2 tbs. chopped onion
2 tsp. olive oil
1 tbs. unsalted butter
3 eggs
3 tbs. water
1/8 tsp. salt
1/8 tsp. black pepper
1/4 cup shredded mozzarella cheese
1/4 cup warm spaghetti sauce

In a small skillet over medium heat, add the mushrooms, onion and olive oil. Saute for 5 minutes. Remove the vegetables from the skillet and set aside for the moment.

Add the butter to the skillet. In a small bowl, add the eggs, water, salt and black pepper. Whisk until combined. When the butter melts, add the eggs. Do not stir. When the edges of the omelet are set, lift the edges to allow the uncooked eggs to run underneath. Cook for 3 minutes or until the omelet is set.

Sprinkle the mozzarella cheese over one half of the omelet. Spread the vegetables over the cheese. Fold the other half of the omelet over the filling. Spoon the spaghetti sauce over the top. Remove the skillet from the heat and serve.

Goat Cheese & Tomato Omelet

Makes 2 servings

3 egg whites
2 eggs
1 tbs. water
1/8 tsp. salt
1/8 tsp. black pepper
1/3 cup crumbled goat cheese
1 plum tomato, diced
2 tbs. chopped fresh basil

In a mixing bowl, add the egg whites, eggs, water, salt and black pepper. Whisk until well combined. Spray an 8" skillet with non stick cooking spray. Place the skillet over medium heat. Add the eggs to the skillet. Do not stir.

As the edges of the eggs set, lift the edges of the omelet with a spatula to let the uncooked eggs run underneath. When the center of the omelet is almost set, sprinkle the goat cheese, tomato and basil over the omelet. Using a spatula, fold the omelet over the filling. Place a lid on the skillet and cook for 1 minute or until the omelet is set and the filling ingredients hot. Remove the skillet from the heat and serve.

Oven Baked Denver Omelet

Makes 6 servings

8 eggs
1 cup whole milk
1/2 tsp. season salt
2 cups frozen shredded hashbrowns
1 cup diced cooked ham
1 cup shredded cheddar cheese
1 tbs. dried minced onion

Preheat the oven to 350°. Spray an 8" square baking pan with non stick cooking spray. In a mixing bowl, add the eggs, milk and season salt. Whisk until combined. Add the hashbrowns, ham, cheddar cheese and onion. Whisk until combined and pour into the pan.

Bake for 35 minutes or until a knife inserted off center of the omelet comes out clean. Remove the omelet from the oven and serve.

French Potato Omelets

Makes 3 servings

3/4 lb. new potatoes
1 1/4 tsp. salt
3 tbs. unsalted butter
1/4 tsp. black pepper
6 eggs
3 tbs. water
2 tbs. chopped fresh chives

In a sauce pan over medium heat, add the potatoes and 1 teaspoon salt. Cover the potatoes with water and bring the potatoes to a boil. Cook for 15 minutes or until the potatoes are tender. Remove the pan from the heat and drain all the water from the potatoes. Cool the potatoes for 15 minutes.

Cube the potatoes. In an 8" skillet over medium heat, add 2 tablespoons butter. When the butter melts, add the potatoes, 1/4 teaspoon salt and black pepper. Cook for 6 minutes or until the potatoes are golden brown. Remove the potatoes from the skillet and set aside.

In a mixing bowl, add the eggs, water and chives. Whisk until well blended. Add 1 tablespoon butter to the skillet. When the butter melts, add the eggs. Do not stir. As the edges of the eggs set, lift the edges of the omelet with a spatula to let the uncooked eggs run underneath. When the center of the omelet is almost set, sprinkle the potatoes over the omelet. Using a spatula, fold the omelet over the filling. Place a lid on the skillet and cook for 1 minute or until the omelet is set and the potatoes hot. Remove the skillet from the heat and serve.

Spinach Red Pepper Omelet

Makes 1 serving

1 egg
2 egg whites
2 tbs. chopped fresh spinach
1/8 tsp. Tabasco sauce
2 tbs. chopped red bell pepper
1 green onion, chopped
2 tbs. shredded cheddar cheese

In a small bowl, add the egg, egg whites, spinach and Tabasco sauce. Whisk until combined. Spray a small skillet with non stick cooking spray. Place the skillet over medium heat. When the skillet is hot, add the red bell pepper and green onion. Saute for 4 minutes.

Add the eggs to the skillet. Do not stir. As the edges of the omelet set, gently lift up the edges to allow the uncooked eggs to run underneath. Cook for 2-3 minutes or until the eggs are set. Sprinkle the cheddar cheese over the omelet. Remove the skillet from the heat. Fold the omelet in half and serve.

Spinach & Cheese Omelet

Makes 1 serving

2 eggs
2 tbs. water
1 tbs. unsalted butter
1 cup chopped fresh spinach
1/3 cup chopped fresh tomato
1/8 tsp. salt
1/3 cup shredded Swiss cheese
1/8 tsp. black pepper

In a small bowl, add the eggs and water. Whisk until combined. In an 8" skillet over medium heat, add the butter. When the butter melts, add the spinach and tomato. Saute for 1 minute. Add the eggs to the skillet. Do not stir. Sprinkle the salt over the eggs.

As the omelet sets on the bottom and edges, gently lift the edges to allow the uncooked eggs to run underneath. Place a lid on the skillet and cook for 1-2 minutes or until the omelet is set. Sprinkle the Swiss cheese and black pepper over the omelet. Fold the omelet in half. Remove the skillet from the heat and serve.

Mushroom Omelet

Makes 2 servings

4 fresh mushrooms, sliced
1/8 tsp. caraway seeds
1/8 tsp. lemon pepper seasoning
1 tbs. unsalted butter
3 eggs
2 tbs. whole milk
1/8 tsp. salt
1/8 tsp. black pepper

In an 8" skillet over medium heat, add the mushrooms, caraway seeds, lemon pepper seasoning and butter. Saute for 5 minutes or until the mushrooms are tender.

In a small bowl, add the eggs, milk, salt and black pepper. Whisk until combined and pour over the mushrooms. Do not stir. As the edges of the eggs set, lift the edges of the omelet with a spatula to let the uncooked eggs run underneath. Using a spatula, fold the omelet in half. Place a lid on the skillet and cook for 2 minutes or until the omelet is set. Remove the skillet from the heat and serve.

Deluxe Ham Omelet

Makes 2 servings

3 eggs
2 tbs. half and half
2 tbs. minced fresh chives
1/2 tsp. garlic salt
1/4 tsp. black pepper
1 tbs. olive oil
1/2 cup chopped cooked ham
2 tbs. chopped green bell pepper
2 tbs. chopped fresh tomato
2 fresh mushrooms, sliced
2 tbs. shredded cheddar cheese
2 tbs. shredded mozzarella cheese

In a small bowl, add the eggs, half and half, chives, garlic salt and black pepper. Whisk until well combined. In a skillet over medium heat, add the olive oil. When the oil is hot, add the eggs. Do not stir.

As the edges of the eggs set, lift the edges of the omelet with a spatula to let the uncooked eggs run underneath. When the center of the omelet is almost set, sprinkle the ham, green bell pepper, tomato, mushrooms, cheddar cheese and mozzarella cheese over one side of the omelet. Using a spatula, fold the omelet over the filling. Place a lid on the skillet and cook for 2 minutes or until the omelet is set and the filling ingredients hot. Remove the skillet from the heat and serve.

Cheddar, Ham & Green Onion Baked Omelet

Makes 12 servings

16 eggs
2 cups whole milk
2 cups shredded cheddar cheese
1 cup cubed cooked ham
6 green onions, chopped

Spray a 9 x 13 baking pan with non stick cooking spray. Preheat the oven to 350°. In a mixing bowl, add all the ingredients. Whisk until combined and pour into the pan.

Bake for 40-45 minutes or until the omelet is set in the center. Remove from the oven and cool for 5 minutes before serving.

Hot & Spicy Omelet

Makes 4 servings

8 eggs
2 tbs. water
4 garlic cloves, minced
1/2 tsp. salt
1/4 tsp. black pepper
1 tbs. vegetable oil
1 tbs. unsalted butter
1/4 tsp. crushed red pepper flakes

In a mixing bowl, add the eggs, water, garlic, salt and black pepper. Whisk until well combined. In a large skillet over medium heat, add the vegetable oil and butter. When the butter melts, add the eggs. Do not stir.

As the edges of the eggs set, lift the edges of the omelet with a spatula to let the uncooked eggs run underneath. Cook until the omelet is set but still moist. Using a spatula, fold the omelet. Sprinkle the omelet with the red pepper flakes. Remove the skillet from the heat and serve.

Spicy Bacon Omelet

Makes 1 omelet

2 eggs
2 tbs. water
2 tsp. minced fresh chives
4 drops Tabasco sauce
Salt and black pepper to taste
2 bacon slices, cooked and crumbled
1 tbs. unsalted butter

In a small bowl, add the eggs, water, chives and Tabasco sauce. Whisk until combined. Season to taste with salt and black pepper. Add the bacon and whisk until combined.

In an 8" skillet over medium heat, add the butter. When the butter melts, add the eggs. Do not stir. As the edges of the eggs set, lift the edges of the omelet with a spatula to let the uncooked eggs run underneath. Cook until the omelet is set but still moist. Using a spatula, fold the omelet. Remove the skillet from the heat and serve.

Southwestern Omelet

Makes 4 servings

1/2 cup chopped onion
1 jalapeno pepper, seeded and minced
1 tbs. vegetable oil
6 beaten eggs
Salt and black pepper to taste
6 bacon slices, cooked and crumbled
1 cup diced fresh tomato
1 avocado, cut into 1" slices
1 cup shredded Monterey Jack cheese
Salsa to taste

In a skillet over medium heat, add the onion, jalapeno pepper and vegetable oil. Saute the vegetables for 5 minutes. Remove the onion and jalapeno pepper from the skillet using a slotted spoon. Set aside on paper towels to drain.

Add the eggs to the skillet. Do not stir. Season the eggs with salt and black pepper to taste. As the edges of the eggs set, lift the edges of the omelet with a spatula to let the uncooked eggs run underneath. Cook until the omelet is set but still moist.

Spoon the onion, jalapeno pepper, bacon, tomato, avocado and 1/2 cup Monterey Jack cheese over the omelet. Using a spatula, fold the omelet over the filling. Place a lid on the skillet and let the omelet cook for 2 minutes. Remove the skillet from the heat and sprinkle 1/2 cup Monterey Jack cheese over the top. Serve with salsa to taste.

Asian Dinner Omelet

This is a great recipe for dinner on a budget.

Makes 6 servings

2 pkgs. ramen noodles, 3 oz. size
1/2 cup thinly sliced celery
2 tsp. vegetable oil
8 oz. pkg. sliced fresh mushrooms
4 tbs. green onions, thinly sliced
2 tbs. minced fresh ginger
3 eggs
6 egg whites
1 tsp. sesame oil
1/2 tsp. granulated sugar
1/2 tsp. salt
2 tbs. soy sauce

Discard the seasoning packet from the ramen noodles. Add the noodles to a pan over medium heat. Cover the noodles with water and bring to a boil. Cook for 3 minutes or until the noodles are tender. Remove the pan from the heat and drain all the water from the noodles.

In a 10" oven proof skillet over medium heat, add the celery and vegetable oil. Saute for 3 minutes. Add the mushrooms, 2 tablespoons green onions and ginger to the skillet. Saute for 6 minutes or until the mushrooms are lightly browned. Remove the skillet from the heat. Add the noodles to the skillet and stir until combined.

In a mixing bowl, add the eggs, egg whites, sesame oil, granulated sugar and salt. Whisk until combined. Add the noodles and vegetables from the skillet to the eggs. Stir until combined. Spread the omelet back into the skillet and place over medium heat. Cook for 2 minutes and remove from the heat.

Preheat the oven to 350°. Bake for 10 minutes or until the omelet is set in the center. Remove from the oven. Sprinkle 2 tablespoons green onions over the omelet. Drizzle the soy sauce over the top and serve.

Strawberry Banana Omelet

This omelet is so much better than you think it will be!

Makes 2 servings

3 tbs. unsalted butter
2 tbs. light brown sugar
1/8 tsp. ground cinnamon
2 ripe bananas, peeled & diced
1/4 tsp. vanilla extract
1 1/2 cups sliced fresh strawberries
6 eggs
2 tbs. water
1/2 tsp. salt
Powdered sugar, optional

In a sauce pan over medium heat, add 1 tablespoon butter. When the butter melts, add the brown sugar and cinnamon. Stir constantly and cook until the brown sugar dissolves. Add the bananas and vanilla extract to the pan. Toss until the bananas are coated in the sauce. Remove the pan from the heat and stir in the strawberries.

In a 10" skillet over medium heat, add 2 tablespoons butter. In a mixing bowl, add the eggs, water and salt. Whisk until combined. When the butter melts, add the eggs. Do not stir. When the bottom and edges of the eggs are set, gently lift up the edges to allow the uncooked eggs to run underneath.

Cook for 2-3 minutes or until the omelet is set. Spoon 2/3 of the fruit over one half of the omelet. Fold the remaining omelet over the top. Cook for 1 minute. Remove from the skillet and slide the omelet onto a serving plate. Spoon the remaining fruit over the top and serve.

Strawberry Bliss Omelet

We love this omelet for a quick dinner. It's like having an omelet and French toast without the bread.

Makes 2 servings

6 eggs
2 tbs. water
1/2 tsp. salt
1/8 tsp. black pepper
2 tbs. unsalted butter
2 oz. cream cheese, cut into cubes
3 tbs. light brown sugar
1 1/2 cups sliced fresh strawberries
Powdered sugar to taste

In a small bowl, add the eggs, water, salt and black pepper. Whisk until combined. In a 10" skillet over medium heat, add the butter. When the butter melts, add the eggs. Do not stir. When the eggs set around the edges, gently lift up the edges to let the uncooked eggs run underneath. Cook for 3 minutes or until the eggs are almost set.

Place the cream cheese cubes over one half of the omelet. Sprinkle the brown sugar over the cream cheese. Spread 1 cup strawberries over the cream cheese. Fold the other half of the omelet over the filling.

Cook for 1-2 minutes or until the omelet is set and the brown sugar melts. Remove the skillet from the heat and slide the omelet onto a serving platter. Spoon 1/2 cup strawberries over the top. Sprinkle powdered sugar to taste over the omelet and serve.

Ham & Avocado Egg Scramble

Makes 4 servings

8 eggs
1/4 cup whole milk
1 tsp. garlic powder
1/4 tsp. black pepper
1 cup cubed cooked ham
1 tbs. unsalted butter
1 ripe avocado, peeled, pitted & cubed
1 cup shredded Colby Jack cheese

In a mixing bowl, add the eggs, milk, garlic powder and black pepper. Whisk until combined and add the ham. Stir until combined. In a skillet over medium heat, add the butter. When the butter melts, add the eggs. Stir constantly and cook until the eggs are almost set.

Add the avocado and Colby Jack cheese to the skillet. Stir until combined and the eggs are set. Remove from the heat and serve.

Spinach Mushroom Scrambled Eggs

Makes 2 servings

2 eggs
2 egg whites
1/8 tsp. salt
1/8 tsp. black pepper
1 tsp. unsalted butter
1/2 cup sliced fresh mushrooms
1/2 cup chopped fresh baby spinach
2 tbs. shredded provolone cheese

In a small bowl, add the eggs, egg whites, salt and black pepper. Whisk until combined. In a skillet over medium heat, add the butter. When the butter melts, add the mushrooms. Saute for 4 minutes. Add the spinach to the skillet. Saute for 2 minutes.

Add the eggs to the skillet. Stir frequently and cook until the eggs are set and scrambled. Sprinkle the provolone cheese over the top. Remove the skillet from the heat and serve.

Tex Mex Scramble

Makes 2 servings

3 corn tortillas, 6" size
4 tsp. olive oil
2 tbs. chopped onion
1 jalapeno pepper, seeded & chopped
4 beaten eggs
1 plum tomato, diced
1/4 cup shredded cooked roast beef
1/8 tsp. salt
1/8 tsp. black pepper
1/4 cup shredded Monterey Jack cheese

Cut the tortillas into thin strips. In a skillet over medium heat, add the corn tortilla strips and 2 teaspoons olive oil. Saute for 4 minutes or until the tortillas are browned but not crisp. Add the onion and jalapeno pepper to the skillet. Saute for 2 minutes.

Add 2 teaspoons olive oil, eggs, tomato, roast beef, salt and black pepper to the skillet. Stir frequently and cook until the eggs are completely set. Sprinkle the Monterey Jack cheese over the top. Remove the skillet from the heat and let the cheese melt for 2 minutes before serving.

Tex Mex Migas

Makes 2 servings

1/4 cup chopped onion
1/4 cup chopped green bell pepper
1 tbs. bacon drippings
4 eggs
1 tbs. water
1 tbs. salsa
1/2 cup crushed tortilla chips
1/2 cup shredded cheddar cheese
2 tbs. chopped green onions
Additional salsa to taste

In a skillet over medium heat, add the onion, green bell pepper and bacon drippings. Saute for 4 minutes. In a small bowl, add the eggs, water and 1 tablespoon salsa. Whisk until combined and add to the skillet. Stir frequently and cook until the eggs are almost set and scrambled. Stir in the tortilla chips and 1/4 cup cheddar cheese.

Cook about 1 minute or until the eggs are set. Remove the skillet from the heat. Sprinkle 1/4 cup cheddar cheese and the green onions over the top. Spoon salsa to taste over the top.

Cream Cheese Basil Scrambled Eggs

Makes 4 servings

8 eggs
1/4 cup whole milk
1/2 tsp. salt
1/2 tsp. black pepper
1 tbs. unsalted butter
3 oz. cream cheese, cubed
1/2 cup chopped fresh basil

In a mixing bowl, add the eggs, milk, salt and black pepper. Whisk until well combined. Add the butter to a skillet over medium heat. When the butter melts, add the eggs. Do not stir until the eggs begin to set on the bottom. Sprinkle the cream cheese over the eggs. Stir frequently and cook until the eggs are set but still moist. Remove the skillet from the heat and stir in the fresh basil. Serve immediately.

Curry Egg Scramble

Makes 4 servings

8 eggs
1/4 cup whole milk
1/2 tsp. curry powder
1/4 tsp. salt
1/8 tsp. black pepper
1/8 tsp. ground cardamom
2 tomatoes, chopped

In a mixing bowl, add the eggs, milk, curry powder, salt, black pepper and cardamom. Whisk until combined. Spray a large non stick skillet with non stick cooking spray. Place the skillet over medium heat. When the skillet is hot, add the eggs.

Stir frequently and cook about 4 minutes or until the eggs are set and scrambled. Remove the skillet from the heat and sprinkle the tomatoes over the top.

Calico Scrambled Eggs

Makes 4 servings

8 eggs
1/4 cup whole milk
1/8 tsp. dried dill
1/4 tsp. salt
1/4 tsp. black pepper
1 tbs. unsalted butter
1/2 cup chopped green bell pepper
1/4 cup chopped onion
1/2 cup chopped fresh tomato

In a mixing bowl, add the eggs, milk, dill, salt and black pepper. Whisk until combined. In a 12" skillet over medium heat, add the butter. When the butter melts, add the green bell pepper and onion. Saute for 4 minutes.

Add the eggs to the skillet. Stir frequently and cook until the eggs are set and scrambled. Stir in the tomatoes. Remove the skillet from the heat and serve.

Bacon & Potato Scrambled Eggs

Makes 4 servings

8 bacon slices, diced
2 cups diced red potatoes
1/2 cup chopped onion
1/2 cup chopped green bell pepper
8 eggs
1/4 cup whole milk
1 tsp. salt
1/4 tsp. black pepper
1 cup shredded cheddar cheese

In a skillet over medium heat, add the bacon. Cook about 5 minutes or until the bacon is crispy. Remove the bacon from the skillet using a slotted spoon. Drain the bacon on paper towels.

Add the potatoes to the skillet. Stir frequently and cook about 12-15 minutes or until the potatoes are tender. Add the onion and green bell pepper to the skillet. Saute for 4 minutes. Add the bacon to the skillet.

In a mixing bowl, add the eggs, milk, salt and black pepper. Whisk until combined and add to the skillet. Stir frequently and cook until the eggs are scrambled and set. Sprinkle the cheddar cheese over the top of the eggs. Remove the skillet from the heat and serve.

Southwest Tortilla Scramble

Makes 2 servings

4 egg whites
2 eggs
1/4 tsp. black pepper
2 corn tortillas, 6" size
1/4 cup chopped fresh spinach
2 tbs. shredded cheddar cheese
1/4 cup salsa

In a mixing bowl, add the egg whites, eggs and black pepper. Whisk until combined. Tear the tortillas in half and cut into thin strips. Add the tortillas to the bowl. Add the spinach and cheddar cheese to the bowl. Stir until combined.

Spray a large skillet with non stick cooking spray. Place the skillet over medium heat. Pour the eggs into the skillet. Once the eggs are set on the bottom, stir until the eggs are scrambled and set. Remove from the heat and spoon the salsa over the top of the eggs.

Green Onion & Cream Cheese Scrambled Eggs

Makes 3 servings

6 eggs
1/2 cup whole milk
3 oz. cream cheese, cubed
1/4 tsp. salt
1/8 tsp. black pepper
4 green onions, chopped
3 tbs. unsalted butter

Add the eggs, milk, cream cheese, salt and black pepper to a blender. Process until smooth and combined. Turn the blender off and stir in the green onions.

Add the butter to a skillet over medium heat. When the butter melts, add the eggs. Do not stir until the eggs begin to set on the bottom. Stir frequently and cook until the eggs are set but still moist. Remove the skillet from the heat and serve.

Haystack Eggs

Makes 4 servings

1 1/2 oz. can shoestring potatoes
4 eggs
1 cup shredded cheddar cheese
6 bacon slices, cooked and crumbled
1 tbs. finely chopped fresh parsley

Preheat the oven to 350°. Spray an 8" square baking pan with non stick cooking spray. Spread the shoestring potatoes in the bottom of the baking pan. Make 4 indentations in the potatoes with the back of a spoon large enough for the eggs.

Break an egg into each indentation. Bake for 8 minutes. Sprinkle the cheddar, cheese, bacon and parsley over the eggs. Bake for 5 minutes or until the eggs are set. Remove the pan from the oven and serve.

You can substitute fried shoestring french fried potatoes if desired.

Bacon Cheddar Egg Scramble

Makes 2 servings

1/4 cup chopped onion
1/4 cup chopped green bell pepper
1 tbs. melted unsalted butter
4 beaten eggs
2 tbs. whole milk
1/8 tsp. season salt
4 bacon slices, cooked and crumbled
1/4 cup shredded cheddar cheese

In a skillet over medium heat, add the onion, green bell pepper and butter. Saute for 5 minutes. In a mixing bowl, add the eggs, milk and season salt. Whisk until combined and add to the skillet.

Do not stir until the eggs begin to set on the bottom. Sprinkle the bacon and cheddar cheese over the eggs. Stir frequently and cook until the eggs are set but still moist. Remove the skillet from the heat and serve.

Mexican Scrambled Eggs

Makes 6 servings

8 beaten eggs
1 tomato, peeled, seeded and chopped
1 tbs. finely chopped jalapeno pepper
1 tbs. chopped fresh cilantro
2 tbs. whole milk
1/4 tsp. ground cumin
1/4 tsp. salt
1/8 tsp. black pepper
2 tbs. unsalted butter
1/2 cup chopped ham

In a mixing bowl, add the eggs, tomato, jalapeno pepper, cilantro, milk, cumin, salt and black pepper. Whisk until combined. In a skillet over medium heat, add the butter. When the butter melts, add the ham. Saute for 2 minutes.

Add the eggs to the skillet. Do not stir until the eggs begin to set on the bottom. Stir frequently and cook until the eggs are set but still moist. Remove the skillet from the heat and serve.

Salmon Scramble

Makes 4 servings

8 eggs
3/4 cup whole milk
1/2 tsp. salt
1/8 tsp. black pepper
7 oz. can pink salmon, drained
1/2 cup shredded Monterey Jack cheese
1/4 cup minced fresh parsley
2 tbs. unsalted butter

In a small bowl, add the eggs, milk, salt and black pepper. Whisk until combined. Remove the skin and bones from the salmon. Add the salmon, Monterey Jack cheese and parsley to the eggs. Whisk until combined.

In a skillet over medium heat, add the butter. When the butter melts, add the eggs. Do not stir until the eggs begin to set on the bottom. Stir frequently and cook until the eggs are set but still moist. Remove the skillet from the heat and serve.

Corn Scrambled Eggs

Makes 3 servings

6 eggs
14 oz. can cream style corn
8 oz. bacon, cooked and crumbled
2 tbs. unsalted butter

In a mixing bowl, add the eggs, corn and bacon. Whisk until well combined. Add the butter to a 9" skillet over medium heat. When the butter melts, add the eggs.

Do not stir until the eggs begin to set on the bottom. Using a wide spatula, run the spatula along the bottom of the skillet. Continue stirring until the eggs are set but still moist. Remove the skillet from the heat and serve.

Mexican Corn Scramble

Makes 6 servings

1/2 cup chopped onion
3 tbs. unsalted butter
11 oz. can Mexicorn, drained
1/4 cup sliced black olives
8 beaten eggs
1 cup hot & cooked sausage crumbles
3/4 cup shredded cheddar cheese

In a large skillet over medium heat, add the onion and butter. Saute the onion for 4 minutes. Add the Mexicorn and black olives. Stir until combined. Add the eggs to the skillet.

Do not stir until the eggs begin to set on the bottom. Using a wide spatula, run the spatula along the bottom of the skillet. Continue stirring until the eggs are set but still moist. Add the sausage and cheddar cheese to the skillet. Stir until combined. Remove the skillet from the heat and serve.

Savory Topped Bacon Scrambled Eggs

Makes 4 servings

1/4 cup chopped green bell pepper
1 tbs. unsalted butter
8 eggs
10.75 oz. can cream of chicken soup
3/4 tsp. salt
1/2 tsp. black pepper
6 bacon slices, cooked and crumbled
1/2 cup whole milk

In a skillet over medium heat, add the green bell pepper and butter. Saute for 4 minutes. In a mixing bowl, add the eggs, 1/2 cup cream of chicken soup, salt and black pepper. Whisk until combined and add to the skillet.

Do not stir until the eggs begin to set on the bottom. Using a wide spatula, run the spatula along the bottom of the skillet. Continue stirring until the eggs are set but still moist. Add the bacon and stir until combined. Remove the skillet from the heat and spoon the eggs onto a serving platter.

In a microwavable bowl, add the remaining cream of chicken soup and milk. Whisk until combined. Microwave for 1 minute or until the soup is thoroughly heated. Remove the bowl from the microwave and spoon over the top of the eggs.

Mushroom Onion Breakfast Scramble

Makes 6 servings

1 cup chopped purple onion
1 cup chopped green bell pepper
4 oz. jar sliced mushrooms, drained
5 tbs. unsalted butter
12 eggs
3/4 cup half and half
1 1/2 tsp. salt
1/4 tsp. black pepper
1 1/2 cups shredded cheddar cheese
1 tbs. minced fresh chives

In a skillet over medium heat, add the purple onion, green bell pepper, mushrooms and butter. Saute for 5 minutes or until the vegetables are tender.

In a mixing bowl, add the eggs, half and half, salt and black pepper. Whisk until combined and add to the skillet. Do not stir until the eggs begin to set on the bottom. Using a wide spatula, run the spatula along the bottom of the skillet. Continue stirring until the eggs are set but still moist. Remove the skillet from the heat and sprinkle the cheddar cheese and chives over the eggs before serving.

Sausage Breakfast Hash

Makes 4 servings

3 tbs. unsalted butter
20 oz. pkg. refrigerated diced potatoes with onion
8 oz. cooked breakfast sausage links, sliced
1/2 cup green bell pepper, chopped
1/2 cup red bell pepper, chopped
1/4 tsp. salt
1/8 tsp. cayenne pepper
1 cup shredded Swiss cheese
8 eggs
Salt and black pepper to taste
Tabasco sauce to taste

In a large skillet over medium heat, add 1 tablespoon butter. When the butter melts, add the potatoes, sausage, green bell peppers, red bell peppers, salt and cayenne pepper. Stir frequently and cook for 12 minutes or until the potatoes are browned. Sprinkle the Swiss cheese over the the top of the potatoes. Remove the skillet from the heat and spoon the potatoes and sausage onto a serving platter.

You will need to cook the eggs in batches. Add 1 tablespoon butter to a skillet over medium heat. When the butter melts and the skillet is hot, break 4 eggs into the skillet. Season to taste with salt and black pepper. Cook for 2 minutes or until the eggs are set. Flip the eggs over and cook for 30 seconds or until the eggs are done to your taste. Remove the eggs from the skillet and place the eggs over the potatoes and sausage. Repeat until all the eggs are cooked. Season to taste with Tabasco sauce.

Barbecue Chicken Polenta With Fried Eggs

Makes 4 servings

2 cups shredded cooked chicken breast
3/4 cup barbecue sauce
1 tbs. minced fresh cilantro
2 tbs. olive oil
1 lb. tube polenta, cut into 8 slices
1 garlic clove, minced
4 eggs
Salt and black pepper to taste

In a small sauce pan over medium heat, add the chicken, barbecue sauce and cilantro. Stir until combined and bring to a boil. Remove the pan from the heat and keep warm while you prepare the rest of the dish.

In a large skillet over medium heat, add 1 tablespoon olive oil. When the oil is hot, add the polenta slices. Sprinkle the garlic over the polenta slices. Cook for 3 minutes on each side or until golden brown. Remove the polenta from the skillet and place two polenta slices on each serving plate. Keep warm while you prepare the eggs.

Reduce the heat to low. Add 1 tablespoon olive oil to the skillet. When the oil is hot, break the eggs into the skillet. Season to taste with salt and black pepper. Cook for 2 minutes or until the eggs are set. Flip the eggs over and cook for 30 seconds. Remove the skillet from the heat.

Place one egg over the polenta slices on each plate. Spoon the barbecue chicken over the top and serve.

Huevos Rancheros With Tomatillo Sauce

Makes 8 servings

5 tomatillos, husked & halved
2 tbs. chopped onion
1 serrano pepper, halved
3 garlic cloves, peeled
1 tsp. instant chicken bouillon granules
15 oz. can seasoned black beans
8 eggs
4 oz. Manchego cheese, shredded
8 tostada shells, warmed
1/2 cup sour cream

Add the tomatillos, onion, serrano pepper, garlic and chicken bouillon to a food processor. Pulse until finely chopped. Add the black beans with liquid to a microwavable bowl. Using a fork, mash until mostly smooth. Microwave for 2 minutes or until the beans are hot. Remove from the microwave.

Spray a large skillet with non stick cooking spray. Place the skillet over low heat. When the skillet is hot, break 4 eggs into the skillet. Place a lid on the skillet. Cook for 5 minutes or until the eggs are cooked to your taste and set. Sprinkle half the Manchego cheese over the eggs. Remove the eggs from the skillet. Repeat this step until all the eggs are cooked.

Spread the beans over one side of each tostada shell and place on serving plates. Place one egg over the beans. Spoon the tomatillo sauce over the top. Spoon a dollop of sour cream over the eggs and serve.

Denver Scrambled Egg Tostadas

Makes 6 servings

1 tbs. unsalted butter
1/2 cup finely chopped green bell pepper
1/3 cup chopped onion
1/4 tsp. black pepper
1/8 tsp. salt
12 beaten eggs
1 cup cubed cooked ham
3/4 cup shredded cheddar cheese
6 warm tostada shells

In a large skillet over medium heat, add the butter. When the butter melts, add the green bell pepper, onion, black pepper and salt. Saute for 5 minutes. Add the eggs and ham to the skillet. Stir frequently and cook until the eggs are set and scrambled. Remove the skillet from the heat. Sprinkle the cheddar cheese over the eggs. Spoon the eggs over the tostadas and serve.

Vegetable Scrambled Eggs

Makes 4 servings

8 eggs
1/2 cup whole milk
1 cup chopped green bell pepper
1/2 cup sliced green onion
1 tsp. salt
1/4 tsp. black pepper
2 tbs. unsalted butter
2 fresh tomatoes, diced

In a small bowl, add the eggs and milk. Whisk until combined. Add the green bell pepper, green onion, salt and black pepper to the eggs. Whisk until combined. In a skillet over medium heat, add the butter. When the butter melts, add the eggs.

Do not stir until the eggs begin to set on the bottom. Using a wide spatula, run the spatula along the bottom of the skillet. Continue stirring until the eggs are set but still moist. Remove the skillet from the heat and sprinkle the tomatoes over the eggs before serving.

Garden Scrambled Eggs

Makes 3 servings

1 cup diced zucchini
1/2 chopped cooked asparagus
1/2 cup shredded carrot
1/4 cup diced red bell pepper
2 green onions, thinly sliced
3 tbs. melted unsalted butter
6 eggs
1/4 cup whole milk
1 tbs. chopped fresh basil
1/2 tsp. salt
1/4 cup shredded Gruyere cheese

In a skillet over medium heat, add the zucchini, asparagus, carrot, red bell pepper, green onions and 2 tablespoons butter. Saute for 7 minutes or until the vegetables are tender. Remove the vegetables from the skillet and set aside.

In a small bowl, add the eggs, milk, basil and salt. Whisk until combined. Add 1 tablespoon butter to the skillet. When the butter melts, add the eggs. Do not stir until the eggs begin to set on the bottom. Spoon the vegetables over the eggs. Sprinkle the Gruyere cheese over the eggs. Stir frequently and cook until the eggs are set but still moist. Remove the skillet from the heat and serve.

2 QUICHES

My family loves quiches. They are quick to prepare and make for a delicious and hearty meal. Most quiches call for a pie crust but I have made them many times without a crust. Spray your pie pan with non stick cooking spray before filling if not using a crust.

Crustless Bacon Mushroom Quiche

Makes 12 servings

10 eggs
1/2 cup all purpose flour
16 oz. container cottage cheese
1/2 cup melted unsalted butter
1 tsp. baking powder
1/4 tsp. salt
4 cups shredded sharp cheddar cheese
15 bacon slices, cooked and crumbled
3 cups sliced fresh mushrooms

Preheat the oven to 350°. Spray a 9 x 13 baking pan with non stick cooking spray. In a mixing bowl, add the eggs. Using a mixer on medium speed, beat until the eggs are foamy. Add the all purpose flour, cottage cheese, butter, baking powder and salt. Mix until combined. Turn the mixer off and stir in 2 cups cheddar cheese, bacon and mushrooms. Spoon into the prepared pan.

Bake for 40 minutes or until the quiche is set in the center. Sprinkle 2 cups cheddar cheese over the top. Bake for 5 minutes or until the cheese melts. Remove the pan from the oven and serve.

Bacon Quiche

Makes 6 servings

9" refrigerated pie crust
1/4 cup sliced green onions
1 tbs. unsalted butter
6 eggs
1 1/2 cups heavy whipping cream
1/4 cup unsweetened apple juice
1 lb. bacon, cooked & crumbled
1/8 tsp. salt
1/8 tsp. black pepper
2 cups shredded Swiss cheese

Preheat the oven to 350°. Place the pie crust in a 9" pie pan. Trim and flute the edges as desired. In a small skillet over medium heat, add the green onions and butter. Saute for 4 minutes and remove the skillet from the heat.

In a mixing bowl, add the eggs, whipping cream and apple juice. Whisk until combined. Add the bacon, green onions, salt and black pepper. Whisk until combined and pour into the pie crust. Sprinkle the Swiss cheese over the top. Bake for 40 minutes or until a knife inserted in the center of the quiche comes out clean. Remove from the oven and cool for 5 minutes before serving.

Canadian Bacon & Onion Quiche

Makes 6 servings

1 cup all purpose flour
3/4 tsp. salt
1/2 cup plus 3 tbs. cold unsalted butter
1/2 cup cottage cheese
6 cups chopped onion
4 oz. Canadian bacon, diced
1/4 tsp. black pepper
3 beaten eggs
1 cup shredded cheddar cheese

Preheat the oven to 350°. In a mixing bowl, add the all purpose flour and 1/4 teaspoon salt. Stir until combined. Add 1/2 cup butter to the bowl. Using a pastry blender, cut the butter into the dry ingredients until you have coarse crumbs. Add the cottage cheese to the bowl. Stir the dough with a fork until the dough leaves the sides of the bowl and forms a ball.

Lightly flour your work surface. Place the dough on your surface. Knead the dough 1 or 2 times so the dough holds together. Roll the dough to a 10" circle and place in a 9" pie pan. Trim and flute the edges as desired.

In a large skillet over medium heat, add the onion and 3 tablespoons butter. Saute for 12 minutes or until the onions are golden brown. Add the Canadian bacon, black pepper and 1/2 teaspoon salt to the skillet. Saute for 3 minutes. Remove the skillet from the heat.

Add the eggs and cheddar cheese to the skillet. Stir until combined and spoon into the pie crust. Bake for 40-45 minutes or until a knife inserted in the center of the quiche comes out clean and the crust is golden brown. Remove from the oven and cool for 5 minutes before serving.

Caramelized Onion Quiche

Makes 6 servings

2 refrigerated pie crust, 9" size
3 large onions, sliced
2 tbs. olive oil
1/2 cup chopped fresh parsley
6 bacon slices, cooked & crumbled
2 cups shredded Gruyere cheese
1 1/2 cups half and half
4 eggs
1/2 tsp. salt
1/4 tsp. black pepper
1/8 tsp. ground nutmeg

Stack the pie crust on top of each other. Lightly flour your work surface. Roll the pie crust to a 12" circle. Place the pie crust in a 10" deep dish tart pan. Trim the edges. Line the pie crust with aluminum foil or pie weights. Preheat the oven to 425°. Bake for 12 minutes. Remove the aluminum foil or pie weights from the crust. Bake for 8 minutes. Remove the crust from the oven and place on a baking sheet.

While the pie crust is cooking, add the onions and olive oil to a large skillet over medium heat. Saute for 15 minutes or until the onions are golden brown. Remove the skillet from the heat and stir in the parsley and bacon. Spread half the onion filling in the tart pan. Sprinkle 1 cup Gruyere cheese over the top. Spread the remaining onion filling over the cheese. Sprinkle 1 cup Gruyere cheese over the onions.

In a mixing bowl, add the half and half, eggs, salt, black pepper and nutmeg. Whisk until combined and pour over the top of the quiche. Do not stir. Bake for 40 minutes or until a knife inserted in the center of the quiche comes out clean. Remove from the oven and cool for 10 minutes before serving.

Roasted Sweet Potato & Onion Quiche

Makes 6-8 servings

3 cups peeled sweet potatoes, cubed
1 cup chopped red onion
2 tbs. olive oil
1 tsp. seasoned pepper blend
6 bacon slices, cooked & crumbled
1/4 cup chopped fresh parsley
2 refrigerated pie crust, 9" size
2 cups shredded Gruyere cheese
1 1/2 cups half and half
4 eggs
1 tsp. chopped fresh rosemary
1/2 tsp. salt

Preheat the oven to 425°. In a mixing bowl, add the sweet potatoes, onion, olive oil and seasoned pepper blend. Toss until the sweet potatoes are coated in the oil and seasoning. Spread the potatoes and onion on a large baking sheet. Bake for 20 minutes or until the sweet potatoes are tender. Stir occasionally while the potatoes cook. Remove from the oven and cool for 10 minutes. Leave the oven on.

Add the sweet potatoes and onion to a mixing bowl. Add the bacon and parsley to the bowl. Toss until combined. Stack the pie crust on top of each other. Lightly flour your work surface. Roll the pie crust to a 12" circle. Place the pie crust in a 10" deep dish tart pan with removable bottom. Trim the edges.

Place heavy duty aluminum foil or pie weights in the pie crust. Bake for 12 minutes. Remove the aluminum foil or pie weights from the crust. Bake for 5 minutes. Remove the crust from the oven and cool completely before filling.

Reduce the oven temperature to 350°. Spread half the sweet potatoes in the bottom of the crust. Sprinkle 1 cup Gruyere cheese over the sweet potatoes. Repeat this layering step one more time. In a mixing bowl, add the half and half, eggs, rosemary and salt. Whisk until combined and pour over the sweet potatoes.

Bake for 35-40 minutes or until a knife inserted in the center of the quiche comes out clean. Remove from the oven and cool for 10 minutes before cutting.

Quesadilla Quiche

Makes 4 servings

2 refrigerated pie crust, 9" size
1 cup chopped onion
1 tbs. unsalted butter
1 cup chopped fresh tomato
1/2 cup sliced black olives
1/4 tsp. garlic salt
1/4 tsp. ground cumin
1/8 tsp. black pepper
4 oz. can diced green chiles, drained
2 beaten eggs
1/8 tsp. Tabasco sauce
1 cup shredded Monterey Jack cheese
1 cup shredded cheddar cheese

Place one pie crust in a 9" pie pan. In a skillet over medium heat, add the onion and butter. Saute for 4 minutes. Add the tomato, black olives, garlic salt, cumin, black pepper and green chiles to the skillet. Stir until combined and cook for 4 minutes. Remove the skillet from the heat.

In a small bowl, add the eggs and Tabasco sauce. Add 1/2 cup Monterey Jack cheese and 1/2 cup cheddar cheese to the eggs. Whisk until combined. Sprinkle 1/2 cup Monterey Jack cheese and 1/2 cup cheddar cheese over the bottom of the pie crust. Spoon the vegetable filling over the cheeses in the pie crust. Pour the eggs over the top. Do not stir but spread the eggs evenly over the filling.

Place the remaining pie crust over the top. Trim and flute the edges as desired. Preheat the oven to 375°. Using a knife, cut several small slits in the top crust to allow the steam to escape. Bake for 45 minutes or until the pie crust is golden brown. Remove from the oven and cool for 5 minutes before cutting.

Mushroom Asparagus Quiche

Makes 6 servings

8 ct. can refrigerated crescent rolls
2 tsp. yellow prepared mustard
1 1/2 lbs. fresh asparagus, trimmed & cut into 1 1/2" pieces
1 cup chopped onion
1 cup sliced fresh mushrooms
1/4 cup unsalted butter, cubed
2 beaten eggs
2 cups shredded mozzarella cheese
1/4 cup minced fresh parsley
1/2 tsp. salt
1/2 tsp. black pepper
1/4 tsp. garlic powder
1/4 tsp. dried basil
1/4 tsp. dried oregano
1/4 tsp. rubbed sage

Preheat the oven to 375°. Remove the crescent dough from the can and place in a 9" pie pan to form a crust. Press any perforations closed. Trim and flute the edges as desired. Brush the mustard over the crust.

In a skillet over medium heat, add the asparagus, onions, mushrooms and butter. Saute for 5 minutes. Remove the skillet from the heat and add the vegetables to a large bowl. Add the eggs, mozzarella cheese, parsley, salt, black pepper, garlic powder, basil, oregano and sage to the bowl. Stir until combined and pour into the crust.

Bake for 25 minutes or until a knife inserted near the center of the quiche comes out clean. Remove from the oven and cool for 5 minutes before serving.

Kentucky Hot Brown Quiche

Makes 8 servings

2 refrigerated pie crust, 9" size
1 1/2 cups chopped cooked turkey
2 cups shredded white cheddar cheese
1/4 cup minced fresh chives
6 bacon slices, cooked & crumbled
1 1/2 cups half and half cream
4 eggs
1/2 tsp. salt
1/4 tsp. black pepper
2 plum tomatoes, cut into 1/4" slices
1/2 cup freshly grated Parmesan cheese

Preheat the oven to 425°. Stack the pie crust on top of each other. Lightly flour your work surface. Roll the pie crust to a 12" circle. Place the pie crust in a 10" deep dish tart pan with removable bottom. Trim the edges.

Place heavy duty aluminum foil or pie weights in the pie crust. Bake for 12 minutes. Remove the aluminum foil or pie weights from the crust. Bake for 5 minutes. Remove the crust from the oven and cool completely before filling. Reduce the oven temperature to 350°.

Spread the turkey in the bottom of the pie crust. Sprinkle the cheddar cheese, chives and bacon over the turkey. In a mixing bowl, add the half and half cream, eggs, salt and black pepper. Whisk until combined and pour over the top of quiche. Do not stir.

Bake for 35 minutes or until the quiche is set in the center. Place the tomatoes over the top of the quiche. Sprinkle the Parmesan cheese over the tomatoes. Bake for 10 minutes. Remove from the oven and cool for 10 minutes before serving.

Bacon Vegetable Quiche

Makes 6 servings

9" refrigerated pie crust
1 cup sliced fresh mushrooms
1 cup chopped fresh broccoli
3/4 cup chopped onion
2 1/2 tsp. olive oil
2 cups fresh baby spinach
3 beaten eggs
5 oz. can evaporated milk
1 tsp. dried rosemary, crushed
1/4 tsp. salt
1/4 tsp. black pepper
1 cup shredded cheddar cheese
6 bacon slices, cooked & crumbled
1/2 cup tomato basil feta cheese

Preheat the oven to 450°. Place the pie crust in a 9" pie pan. Trim and flute the edges as desired. In a skillet over medium heat, add the mushrooms, broccoli, onion and olive oil. Saute for 6 minutes or until the vegetables are tender. Add the spinach to the skillet. Saute for 2 minutes or until the spinach wilts. Remove the skillet from the heat.

In a mixing bowl, add the eggs, evaporated milk, rosemary, salt and black pepper. Whisk until combined. Add the cheddar cheese, vegetables and bacon to the bowl. Whisk until combined and pour into the pie crust. Sprinkle the feta cheese over the top.

Bake for 35 minutes or until a knife inserted in the center of the quiche comes out clean and the pie crust is golden brown. Loosely cover the edges of the pie crust with aluminum foil if the crust is browning too fast. Remove from the oven and cool for 5 minutes before serving.

Ham & Bacon Quiche

Makes 6 servings

9" refrigerated pie crust
6 bacon slices
1/2 cup chopped onion
1 cup sliced fresh mushrooms
1 1/2 cups half and half
1 cup chopped cooked ham
6 beaten eggs
1/2 tsp. season salt
1/2 tsp. black pepper
2 cups shredded Swiss cheese
2 tbs. all purpose flour

Place the pie crust in a 9" pie pan. Trim and flute the edges as desired. Prick the pie crust all over with a fork. Preheat the oven to 400°. Bake for 10 minutes. Remove the pie crust from the oven. Let the pie crust cool while you prepare the filling.

In a large skillet over medium heat, add the bacon. Cook for 8 minutes or until the bacon is crispy. Remove the bacon from the skillet and drain on paper towels. Drain the bacon drippings from the skillet except for 2 tablespoons drippings.

Add the onion and mushrooms to the skillet. Saute for 4 minutes. Remove the skillet from the heat and add the vegetables to a mixing bowl. Crumble the bacon and add to the mixing bowl. Add the half and half, ham, eggs, season salt, black pepper, Swiss cheese and all purpose flour. Whisk until well combined.

Pour the filling into the pie crust. Reduce the oven temperature to 350°. Bake for 40 minutes or until a toothpick inserted in the center of the quiche comes out clean. Remove the quiche from the oven and cool for 5 minutes before serving.

Mini Ham Quiches

Makes 1 dozen

3/4 cup diced cooked ham
1/2 cup shredded sharp cheddar cheese
1/2 cup chopped black olives
3 beaten eggs
1 cup half and half
1/4 cup unsalted butter, melted
3 drops Tabasco sauce
1/2 cup Bisquick
2 tbs. grated Parmesan cheese
1/2 tsp. ground mustard

Spray a 12 count muffin tin with non stick cooking spray. Preheat the oven to 375°. In a small bowl, add the ham, cheddar cheese and black olives. Stir until combined and sprinkle in the bottom of the muffin cups.

In a mixing bowl, add the eggs, half and half, butter, Tabasco sauce, Bisquick, Parmesan cheese and ground mustard. Whisk until combined and pour over the ham in the muffin cups. Bake for 20 minutes or until a knife inserted off center of the quiches comes out clean. Remove the muffin tin from the oven and cool for 5 minutes before serving.

Ham & Cheddar Quiche

Makes 6 servings

1 1/2 cups cubed cooked ham
1 1/2 cups shredded cheddar cheese
1/4 cup chopped onion
3 tbs. chopped green bell pepper
1 cup pancake mix
1/4 tsp. salt
1/8 tsp. black pepper
2 cups whole milk
5 eggs

Preheat the oven to 350°. Spray a shallow 2 quart casserole dish with non stick cooking spray. Sprinkle the ham, cheddar cheese, onion and green bell pepper in the bottom of the casserole dish.

In a mixing bowl, add the pancake mix, salt, black pepper, milk and eggs. Whisk until combined and pour over the ham and vegetables in the pan. Do not stir. Bake for 50 minutes or until a knife inserted in the center of the quiche comes out clean. Remove the quiche from the oven and serve.

Turkey Swiss Quiche

Makes 6 servings

9" refrigerated pie crust
1 1/2 cups finely chopped cooked turkey
4 eggs
3/4 cup half and half cream
2 cups shredded Swiss cheese
4 green onions, finely chopped
2 tbs. diced red pimentos
1 tsp. dried oregano
1 tsp. dried parsley flakes
1/8 tsp. salt
1/8 tsp. black pepper
3 slices Swiss cheese, 1 oz. size

Place the pie crust in a 9" pie pan. Trim and flute the edges as desired. Preheat the oven to 450°. Prick the pie crust all over with a fork. Line the pie crust with heavy duty aluminum foil. Bake for 7 minutes. Remove the aluminum foil from the pie crust. Bake for 4 minutes or until the crust just begins to brown. Remove from the oven. Reduce the oven temperature to 375°.

Sprinkle the turkey in the bottom of the pie crust. In a mixing bowl, add the eggs and half and half. Whisk until combined. Add the shredded Swiss cheese, green onions, red pimentos, oregano, parsley, salt and black pepper. Stir until combined and pour into the pie crust.

Bake for 20 minutes. Cut the slices of Swiss cheese into thin strips. Place the strips over the top of the quiche. Bake for 12-15 minutes or until a knife inserted in the center of the quiche comes out clean. Remove from the oven and cool for 5 minutes before serving.

Asparagus Quiche

Makes 6 servings

9" refrigerated pie crust
10 oz. can asparagus spears, drained
1 cup sliced cooked mushrooms
1 cup shredded Swiss cheese
2 tbs. all purpose flour
3 beaten eggs
1/2 cup half and half
1/2 tsp. salt
1/8 tsp. black pepper
1/8 tsp. ground nutmeg

Preheat the oven to 350°. Place the pie crust in a 9" pie pan. Trim and flute the edges as desired. Place the asparagus and mushrooms over the bottom of the crust.

In a mixing bowl, add the Swiss cheese and all purpose flour. Toss until combined. Add the eggs, half and half, salt, black pepper and nutmeg to the bowl. Whisk until combined and pour into the pie crust.

Bake for 55 minutes or until a knife inserted in the center of the quiche comes out clean. Remove the quiche from the oven and cool for 5 minutes before serving.

Smoked Sausage Crustless Quiche

Makes 6 servings

4 beaten eggs
1/3 cup whole milk
1/4 cup all purpose flour
1/2 tsp. baking powder
1/4 tsp. garlic powder
2 cups shredded cheddar cheese
1 1/2 cups diced smoked sausage
1 cup cottage cheese
1 tbs. minced fresh chives

Preheat the oven to 375°. In a mixing bowl, add the eggs, milk, all purpose flour, baking powder and garlic powder. Whisk until combined. Add 1/1 2 cups cheddar cheese, smoked sausage, cottage cheese and chives. Whisk until combined.

Spray a 9" pie pan with non stick cooking spray. Pour the filling into the pan. Bake for 25 minutes or until a knife inserted in the center of the quiche comes out clean. Remove the quiche from the oven and sprinkle 1/2 cup cheddar cheese over the quiche. Cool for 5 minutes before serving.

Green Vegetable Quiche

Makes 6 servings

1/4 cup olive oil
3 cups fresh broccoli florets
1/2 cup finely chopped onion
3 cups chopped fresh spinach
3 garlic cloves, minced
9" refrigerated pie crust
4 eggs
1 cup whole milk
1 tsp. dried rosemary
1/2 tsp. salt
1/2 tsp. black pepper
1/2 cup shredded cheddar cheese
1/2 cup shredded Swiss cheese

Preheat the oven to 375°. In a large skillet over medium heat, add the olive oil. When the oil is hot, add the broccoli and onion. Saute for 5 minutes. Add the spinach and garlic to the skillet. Saute for 3 minutes or until the spinach wilts. Remove the skillet from the heat.

Place the pie crust in a 9" pie pan. Trim and flute the edges as desired. Spoon the vegetables into the pie crust. In a mixing bowl, add the eggs, milk, rosemary, salt and black pepper. Whisk until combined and stir in 1/4 cup cheddar cheese and 1/4 cup Swiss cheese. Pour the filling into the pie crust. Do not stir.

Sprinkle 1/4 cup cheddar cheese and 1/4 cup Swiss cheese over the top. Bake for 30 minutes or until a knife inserted near the center of the quiche comes out clean. Remove from the oven and cool for 5 minutes before serving.

Pear Pecan Sausage Quiche

Makes 8 servings

8 oz. ground hot Italian sausage
1/3 cup chopped onion
9" refrigerated pie crust
1 pear, peeled, cored & sliced
1/3 cup chopped pecans
4 eggs
1 1/2 cups half and half cream
1/2 tsp. salt
1/2 tsp. dried thyme
1/8 tsp. ground nutmeg
1 cup shredded cheddar cheese
8 pecan halves

In a skillet over medium heat, add the sausage and onion. Stir frequently to break the sausage into crumbles as it cooks. Cook for 8 minutes or until the sausage is well browned and no longer pink. Remove the skillet from the heat and drain off the excess grease.

Place the pie crust in a 9" pie pan. Trim and flute the edges as desired. Place the pear slices in the bottom of the pie crust. Spoon the sausage and chopped pecans over the pears. In a mixing bowl, add the eggs, half and half cream, salt, thyme, nutmeg and cheddar cheese. Whisk until combined and pour over the sausage and pears in the pie crust.

Place the pecan halves over the top. Bake for 35-40 minutes or until a knife inserted in the center of the quiche comes out clean. Remove from the oven and cool for 5 minutes before serving.

Southwestern Quiche

Makes 8 servings

2 refrigerated pie crust, 9" size
2 cups sliced fresh mushrooms
2 tsp. vegetable oil
1/2 cup shredded mozzarella cheese
1/2 cup shredded Swiss cheese
1/2 cup shredded cheddar cheese
5 beaten eggs
1/2 cup half and half
1/2 cup picante sauce
1 tbs. all purpose flour
1/2 cup chopped green bell pepper
1/4 cup sliced black olives, chopped

Stack the pie crust on top of each other. Roll the pie crust together into a 10" circle. Place the pie crust in a 9" pie pan. Flute and trim the edges as desired. Preheat the oven to 425°. Prick the pie crust all over with a fork. Bake for 15 minutes. Remove the pie crust from the oven.

In a skillet over medium heat, add the mushrooms and vegetable oil. Saute for 5 minutes. Remove the skillet from the heat and drain off any excess liquid. In a small bowl, add the mozzarella cheese, Swiss cheese and cheddar cheese. Stir until combined.

In a mixing bowl, add the eggs, half and half, picante sauce and all purpose flour. Whisk until combined. Add the mushrooms, green bell pepper and black olives to the bowl. Stir until combined. Pour half the eggs into the pie crust. Sprinkle 2/3 of the cheeses over the eggs. Spoon the remaining eggs over the top. Sprinkle the remaining cheeses over the eggs.

Preheat the oven to 375°. Bake for 40 minutes or until a toothpick inserted in the center of the quiche comes out clean. Remove the quiche from the oven and cool for 5 minutes before serving.

South Of The Border Breakfast Quiche

Makes 4 servings

4 breakfast sausage patties
8 oz. cream cheese, softened
3 tbs. Bisquick
1 1/4 tsp. sazon con azafran seasoning
1/4 tsp. salt
1/4 tsp. black pepper
1 cup shredded Mexican cheese blend
10 oz. can diced tomatoes with green chiles
7 eggs

In a skillet over medium heat, add the sausage patties. Cook about 4 minutes on each side or until the patties are well browned and no longer pink. Remove the skillet from the heat. Break the patties into small pieces.

Preheat the oven to 350°. Spray an 8" square baking pan with non stick cooking spray. In a mixing bowl, add the cream cheese, Bisquick, sazon con azafran seasoning, salt, black pepper and Mexican cheese blend. Using a mixer on medium speed, beat until well blended. Add the tomatoes with juice and mix until blended. Turn the mixer off.

Add the sausage and eggs to the bowl. Stir until well combined. Spoon the filling into the prepared pan. Bake for 40 minutes or until a toothpick inserted in the center of the quiche comes out clean. Remove the quiche from the oven and cool for 5 minutes before serving.

Cheesy Sausage Quiche

Makes 8 servings

3 cups sliced fresh mushrooms
1/2 cup chopped onion
1 tbs. olive oil
12 oz. ground pork sausage
4 beaten eggs
8 egg whites, beaten
1 cup shredded cheddar cheese
1/2 cup whole milk
1/4 tsp. salt
1/4 tsp. black pepper

In a skillet over medium heat, add the mushrooms, onion and olive oil. Saute for 7 minutes. Remove the vegetables from the skillet and place in a mixing bowl.

Add the sausage to the skillet. Stir frequently to break the sausage into crumbles as it cooks. Cook for 8 minutes or until the sausage is well browned and no longer pink. Remove the skillet from the heat and drain off any excess grease. Spoon the sausage into the mixing bowl with the vegetables.

Add the eggs, egg whites, cheddar cheese, milk, salt and black pepper to the bowl. Whisk until combined. Preheat the oven to 350°. Spray a 10" quiche pan with non stick cooking spray. Spoon the filling into the pan. Bake for 30 minutes or until the center of the quiche is set. Remove the pan from the oven and cool for 10 minutes before serving.

Crab Quiche Bake

Makes 8 servings

8 beaten eggs
2 cups half and half
1 red bell pepper, chopped
8 oz. cooked crabmeat, chopped
1 cup soft breadcrumbs
1 cup shredded Swiss cheese
1 cup shredded cheddar cheese
1/2 cup chopped green onion
1 tsp. salt
1/2 tsp. black pepper

Add all the ingredients to a mixing bowl. Stir until combined. Spray a 9 x 13 baking pan with non stick cooking spray. Spoon the quiche into the baking pan. Preheat the oven to 350°. Bake for 30 minutes or until a knife inserted off center of the quiche comes out clean. Remove the pan from the oven and serve.

Golden Corn Quiche

Makes 8 servings

9" refrigerated pie crust
1 1/3 cups half and half cream
3 eggs
3 tbs. melted unsalted butter
1 cup onion, peeled & cut into thin wedges
1 tbs. all purpose flour
1 tbs. granulated sugar
1 tsp. salt
2 cups frozen whole kernel corn, thawed

Preheat the oven to 375°. Place the pie crust in a 9" pie pan. Trim and flute the edges as desired. Place heavy duty aluminum foil or pie weights over the crust. Bake for 5 minutes. Remove the aluminum foil or pie weights. Bake for 5 minutes and remove from the oven.

In a blender, add the half and half cream, eggs, butter, onion, all purpose flour, granulated sugar and salt. Process until blended. Add the corn to the blender and stir until combined. Pour the filling into the pie crust.

Bake for 35 minutes or until a knife inserted in the center of the quiche comes out clean. Remove from the oven and cool for 5 minutes before serving.

Broccoli Hashbrown Quiche

Makes 6 servings

3 cups shredded frozen hashbrowns, thawed
1 1/2 cups frozen broccoli cuts, thawed
4 eggs
1 cup sour cream
1/2 tsp. salt
1 cup shredded Colby cheese

Preheat the oven to 350°. Spray a 9" square baking pan with non stick cooking spray. Press the hashbrowns in the bottom and up the sides of the pan to form a crust. Sprinkle the broccoli over the hashbrowns.

In a mixing bowl, add the eggs, sour cream, salt and Colby cheese. Whisk until combined and pour over the hashbrowns and broccoli. Bake for 55 minutes or until a knife inserted off center of the quiche comes out clean. Remove from the oven and serve.

Cheesy Vegetable Quiche

Makes 6 servings

9" refrigerated pie crust
1 cup chopped fresh broccoli
1 cup chopped fresh cauliflower
1 1/2 cups shredded cheddar cheese
1 1/2 cups shredded Swiss cheese
4 beaten egg yolks
1 cup whipping cream
1 1/2 tsp. season salt
1/2 tsp. black pepper
1/4 tsp. ground nutmeg

Preheat the oven to 375°. Place the pie crust in a 9" quiche pan. Trim the edges. Prick the bottom and sides of the pie crust with a fork. Bake for 8 minutes. Remove the crust from the oven and cool completely before filling.

In a sauce pan over medium heat, add the broccoli and cauliflower. Cover the vegetables with water. Bring to a boil and cook for 3 minutes. Remove the pan from the heat and drain all the water from the vegetables. Spoon the vegetables into the pie crust.

Sprinkle the cheddar cheese and Swiss cheese over the vegetables. In a mixing bowl, add the egg yolks, whipping cream, season salt, black pepper and nutmeg. Whisk until combined and pour over the vegetables in the pie crust. Do not stir.

Bake for 45 minutes or until a toothpick inserted in the center of the quiche comes out clean. Remove the quiche from the oven and cool for 5 minutes before serving.

Cream Cheese Spinach Quiche

Makes 8 servings

9" refrigerated pie crust
1 tbs. unsalted butter
1/4 cup chopped onion
8 oz. cream cheese, cubed
3/4 cup whole milk
4 eggs, beaten
10 oz. pkg. chopped frozen spinach, thawed
2 oz. jar diced red pimento, drained
1/8 tsp. black pepper

Preheat the oven to 375°. Place the pie crust in a 9" quiche pan. Trim the edges. Prick the bottom and sides of the pie crust with a fork. Bake for 10 minutes. Remove the crust from the oven and cool completely before filling.

In a sauce pan over medium heat, add the butter. When the butter melts, add the onion. Saute for 5 minutes. Add the cream cheese and milk to the skillet. Reduce the heat to low. Stir constantly and cook until the cream cheese melts.

In a small bowl, add the beaten eggs. Add 2 tablespoons milk mixture from the sauce pan to the eggs. Whisk until combined and add to the sauce pan. Stir until well combined. Add the spinach, red pimento and black pepper to the pan. Stir until combined and remove the pan from the heat. Spoon the filling into the pie crust.

Bake for 40 minutes or until a toothpick inserted in the center of the quiche comes out clean. Remove the quiche from the oven and cool for 5 minutes before serving.

Pepperoni Spinach Quiche

Makes 8 servings

8 ct. can refrigerated crescent rolls
1 red bell pepper, chopped
1 garlic clove, minced
1 tbs. olive oil
5 beaten eggs
1/2 cup shredded mozzarella cheese
1/2 cup frozen chopped spinach, thawed & patted dry
1/4 cup sliced pepperoni, cut into thin strips
1/4 cup half and half cream
2 tbs. grated Parmesan cheese
1 tbs. minced fresh parsley
1 tsp. dried basil

Preheat the oven to 375°. Remove the crescent roll dough from the can. Separate the dough into 8 triangles. Press the dough in a 9" tart pan with removable bottom to form a crust. Press any perforations closed with your fingers.

In a skillet over medium heat, add the red bell pepper, garlic and olive oil. Saute for 5 minutes or until the red bell pepper is tender. Remove the skillet from the heat. Add the pepper and garlic to a mixing bowl.

Add the eggs, mozzarella cheese, spinach, pepperoni, half and half cream, Parmesan cheese, parsley and basil to the bowl. Whisk until combined and pour into the crust.

Bake for 25 minutes or until a knife inserted in the center of the quiche comes out clean and the crust is golden brown. Remove from the oven and cool for 5 minutes before serving.

Bacon Quiche Cups

Makes 8 servings

8 oz. pkg. softened cream cheese
2 tbs. whole milk
2 eggs
1/2 cup shredded Swiss cheese
2 tbs. chopped green onion
8 ct. can Grands flaky biscuits
5 bacon slices, cooked and crumbled

Preheat the oven to 375°. In a mixing bowl, add the cream cheese. Using a mixer on medium speed, beat until the cream cheese is smooth and creamy. Add the milk and eggs to the bowl. Mix until blended. Turn the mixer off and stir in the Swiss cheese and green onion.

Remove the biscuits from the can. Press a biscuit in 8 muffin cups forming a crust. Sprinkle half the bacon in the bottom of the crust. Spoon the cream cheese filling over the bacon. Sprinkle the remaining bacon over the filling.

Bake for 20 minutes or until the filling is set and the biscuits are golden brown. Remove the pan from the oven. Cool for 3 minutes and remove the biscuits from the pan. Serve hot.

Cheddar Egg Custard Cups

Makes 4 servings

4 beaten eggs
2 tbs. melted unsalted butter
1 cup whole milk
1 tsp. cornstarch
1/2 tsp. baking powder
1/4 tsp. salt
1/8 tsp. black pepper
1/2 cup shredded cheddar cheese

Preheat the oven to 425°. Spray four 6 oz. custard cups with non stick cooking spray. Place the custard cups in a 9 x 13 baking pan. In a mixing bowl, add all the ingredients. Whisk until combined and pour into the custard cups.

Pour boiling water around the custard cups to a depth of 1” on the custard cups. Bake for 15 minutes or until a knife inserted in the center of the custard comes out clean. Remove from the oven and immediately remove the custard cups from the water. Serve immediately.

Bacon Gruyere Puff Pastry Quiche Cups

Makes 18 miniature quiches

17 oz. pkg. frozen puff pastry, thawed
4 eggs
1 cup plus 2 tbs. half and half cream
1 tbs. minced fresh thyme
1/2 tsp. salt
1/2 tsp. black pepper
1/4 tsp. ground nutmeg
1 1/2 cups shredded Gruyere cheese
1 1/2 cups chopped fresh spinach
1 red bell pepper, chopped
8 bacon slices, cooked & crumbled

Preheat the oven to 400°. Lightly flour your work surface. Place the puff pastry sheets on your work surface. Roll each sheet to a 12" square. Cut each piece into 9 squares. Place the squares in muffin tin cups to form a crust. Let the corners stand up on the puff pastry.

In a mixing bowl, add 3 eggs, 1 cup half and half, thyme, salt, black pepper and nutmeg. Whisk until combined. In a separate bowl, add the Gruyere cheese, spinach, red bell pepper and bacon. Stir until combined. Spoon the cheese mixture into the pastry cups. Spoon the eggs over the cheese mixture. Do not stir.

In a small bowl, add 1 egg and 2 tablespoons half and half. Whisk until combined and brush over the puff pastry edges. Bake for 15-18 minutes or until a toothpick inserted in the quiches comes out clean and the puff pastry is golden brown. Remove from the oven and immediately remove the quiches from the muffin tins. Serve hot.

Broccoli Quiche Crepe Cups

Makes 4 servings

1 3/4 cups whole milk
5 eggs
1 cup all purpose flour
1/4 tsp. salt
10 oz. pkg. frozen broccoli with cheese sauce
3 bacon slices, diced
1/2 cup chopped onion

Add 1 1/2 cups milk, 3 eggs, all purpose flour and salt to a blender. Process until smooth and combined. Spray an 8" skillet with non stick cooking spray. Place the skillet over medium heat. When the skillet is hot, add 2 tablespoons batter in the center of the skillet. Lift and tilt the skillet so the batter covers the bottom of the skillet. Cook for 1-2 minutes or until the top of the crepe looks dry. Flip the crepe over and cook for 30 seconds. Remove the crepe from the skillet. Repeat until all the crepes are made.

Preheat the oven to 350°. You need four crepes for this recipe. Freeze or use the remaining crepes for another recipe. Line four 6 oz. custard cups with a crepe. Add the broccoli with cheese sauce to a microwavable bowl. Microwave for 5-6 minutes or until the broccoli is tender. Remove from the microwave.

In a skillet over medium heat, add the bacon and onion. Cook for 5 minutes or until the bacon is crispy. Remove the skillet from the heat and drain the bacon and onion on paper towels.

In a mixing bowl, add 2 eggs, 1/4 cup milk, bacon and onion along with the broccoli and cheese sauce. Stir until combined and spoon into the crepe cups. Bake for 30 minutes or until a knife inserted in the center of the quiches comes out clean. Remove from the oven and immediately remove the crepes from the custard cups. Serve hot.

Savory Omelet Cups

Makes 4 servings

1/4 cup sun dried tomatoes, not oil packed
1/2 cup water
3 eggs
6 egg whites
2 tbs. minced fresh cilantro
4 tsp. melted unsalted butter
1/2 tsp. salt
1/4 tsp. black pepper
1/3 cup shredded provolone cheese
1 cup chopped leeks, white portion only
2 green onions, chopped
1 tbs. olive oil
2 tbs. chopped kalamata olives
2 tsp. minced fresh oregano
1/4 cup grated Parmesan cheese
1 tbs. honey

In a small bowl, add the sun dried tomatoes and 1/4 cup water. Let the tomatoes sit for 30 minutes. In a mixing bowl, add the eggs, egg whites, 1/4 cup water, cilantro, butter, salt and black pepper. Whisk until combined.

Spray an 8" skillet with non stick cooking spray. Place the skillet over medium heat. When the skillet is hot, add 1/2 cup eggs to the center of the skillet. Lift and tilt the skillet so the eggs coat the bottom of the skillet. Cook for 1-2 minutes or until the top of the crepe looks dry. Flip the crepe over and cook for 30 seconds. Remove from the skillet. Repeat until all the crepes are cooked.

Place the crepes in ramekins to form a crust. Sprinkle the provolone cheese over the crepes. Preheat the oven to 350°. Drain the tomatoes if any water is remaining. Chop the tomatoes.

In a skillet over medium heat, add the leeks, green onions and olive oil. Saute for 5 minutes or until the leeks are tender. Add the tomatoes, olives and oregano to the skillet. Saute for 3 minutes. Remove the skillet from the heat and spoon the vegetables into the crepe cups. Sprinkle the Parmesan cheese over the top. Drizzle the honey over the filling.

Bake for 10 minutes or until the crepe cups are thoroughly heated. Remove from the oven and serve.

3 CASSEROLES & STRATAS

There is nothing easier and tastier to serve for breakfast than casseroles. They can be made ahead for busy mornings. The recipes include a wide variety of flavors sure to please everyone in the family.

Overnight Southwest Breakfast Strata

Makes 6 servings

1 lb. ground pork sausage
1/2 cup chopped onion
1/2 cup chopped green bell pepper
2 cans diced tomatoes with green chiles, 10 oz. size
8 flour tortillas, 10" size
3 cups shredded Colby Jack cheese
6 eggs
2 cups whole milk
1 tsp. salt
1/2 tsp. black pepper

In a large skillet over medium heat, add the sausage. Stir frequently to break the sausage into crumbles as it cooks. Cook for 8 minutes or until the sausage is well browned and no longer pink. Add the onion and green bell pepper to the skillet. Saute the vegetables for 5 minutes. Drain off any excess grease.

Add the tomatoes with juice to the skillet. Stir until combined. Reduce the heat to low and simmer for 10 minutes. Remove the skillet from the heat. Cut the flour tortillas into strips.

Spray a 9 x 13 baking pan with non stick cooking spray. Spread half the tortilla strips in the bottom of the baking pan. Spoon half the sausage mixture over the tortillas. Sprinkle half the Colby Jack cheese over the tortillas. Repeat the layering process one more time.

In a mixing bowl, add the eggs, milk, salt and black pepper. Whisk until combined and pour over the casserole. Do not stir. Lightly cover the pan with aluminum foil and refrigerate the casserole at least 8 hours but not longer than 12 hours.

Remove the casserole from the refrigerator. Let the casserole sit for 30 minutes at room temperature. Remove the aluminum foil from the baking pan. Bake for 30 minutes or until the center of the casserole is set and lightly browned. Remove the pan from the oven and serve.

Slow Cooker Potato Smoked Sausage Casserole

Makes 8 servings

1 lb. smoked sausage, diced
1 cup chopped onion
1 cup chopped red bell pepper
20 oz. pkg. refrigerated O'Brien hashbrowns
1/2 tsp. chili powder
10 eggs
1 cup whole milk
1 cup shredded sharp cheddar cheese

Spray your slow cooker with non stick cooking spray. In a skillet over medium heat, add the smoked sausage, onion and red bell pepper. Saute for 8 minutes or until the smoked sausage is well browned. Remove the skillet from the heat and drain off any grease.

In a mixing bowl, add the hashbrowns and chili powder. Toss until combined. Spoon 1/3 of the potatoes in the bottom of the slow cooker. Spoon half the smoked sausage mixture over the potatoes. Spoon another 1/3 of the potatoes over the smoked sausage. Spoon the remaining smoked sausage over the potatoes. Spoon the remaining potatoes over the smoked sausage.

In a mixing bowl, add the eggs and milk. Whisk until combined and pour over the top of the casserole. Do not stir. Set the slow cooker to low. Cook for 6 hours or until the casserole is set. Sprinkle the cheddar cheese over the top. Let the casserole sit for 10 minutes before serving.

Skillet Breakfast Casserole

Makes 6 servings

3 cups packed shredded potatoes
1 tbs. unsalted butter
2 tbs. vegetable oil
1/2 cup diced red bell pepper
1 cup diced onion
1 garlic clove, minced
3/4 tsp. salt
6 eggs
1/4 tsp. black pepper

Preheat the oven to 350°. Add the shredded potatoes to a large bowl. Cover the potatoes with cold water. Let the potatoes sit for 5 minutes. Drain off all the water and pat the potatoes dry with paper towels.

Add the butter and vegetable oil to a 10" oven proof skillet over medium heat. When the butter melts, add the red bell pepper and onion. Saute for 4 minutes. Add the garlic to the skillet. Saute for 2 minutes. Add the potatoes and 1/2 teaspoon salt to the skillet. Stir frequently and cook for 10 minutes or until the potatoes are golden brown. Remove the skillet from the heat.

Make 6 indentations in the potatoes using the back of a large spoon. Break an egg into each indentation. Sprinkle 1/4 teaspoon salt and the black pepper over the eggs. Bake for 12 minutes or until the eggs are cooked to your taste. Remove the skillet from the oven and serve.

Salami Egg Bake

Makes 8 servings

4 oz. salami, cut into thin strips
2 tbs. finely chopped red onion
6 eggs
1/4 cup whole milk
3 oz. cream cheese, cut into 16 cubes
1 cup mini bagel chips

Preheat the oven to 325°. In a small skillet over medium heat, add the salami and onion. Saute for 3 minutes or until the onion is tender. Remove the skillet from the heat.

In a mixing bowl, add the eggs and milk. Whisk until combined. Lightly spray a 9" pie pan with non stick cooking spray. Pour the eggs into the pie pan. Sprinkle the cream cheese cubes over the eggs. Sprinkle the salami and onion over the top. Place the bagel chips around the edges of the pie pan. Bake for 25-30 minutes or until the eggs are set in the center. Remove from the oven and serve.

BLT Egg Bake

Makes 4 servings

1/4 cup mayonnaise
5 slices toasted bread
4 slices American cheese, 1 oz. size
12 bacon slices, cooked & crumbled
4 eggs
1 tomato, halved & thinly sliced
2 tbs. unsalted butter
2 tbs. all purpose flour
1/4 tsp. salt
1/4 tsp. black pepper
1 cup whole milk
1/2 cup shredded cheddar cheese
2 green onions, thinly sliced
1/2 cup shredded lettuce

Preheat the oven to 325°. Spread the mayonnaise on one side of each toast slice. Cut the toast into small pieces. Spray an 8" square baking pan with non stick cooking spray. Place the toast pieces, mayonnaise side up, in the baking pan. Place the American cheese slices over the toast. Sprinkle the bacon over the top.

Spray a skillet with non stick cooking spray and place over medium heat. When the skillet is hot, break the eggs into the skillet. Cook for 1-2 minutes on each side or until the eggs are done to your taste. Remove the skillet from the heat and place the eggs over the top of the casserole. Place the tomato slices over the eggs.

In a sauce pan over medium heat, add the butter. When the butter melts, stir in the all purpose flour, salt and black pepper. Stir constantly and cook for 1 minute. Add the milk to the pan. Stir constantly and cook about 4 minutes or until the sauce thickens and bubbles. Remove the pan from the heat and pour over the top of the casserole. Sprinkle the cheddar cheese and green onions over the top of the casserole. Bake for 10 minutes. Remove from the oven and sprinkle the lettuce over the top.

Eggs Benedict Casserole

Makes 12 servings

12 oz. Canadian bacon, chopped
6 English muffins, split & cut into 1" pieces
8 eggs
2 cups whole milk
1 tsp. onion powder
1/4 tsp. paprika
4 egg yolks
1/2 cup heavy whipping cream
2 tbs. lemon juice
1 tsp. Dijon mustard
1/2 cup melted unsalted butter

Spray a 9 x 13 baking pan with non stick cooking spray. Spread half the bacon in the bottom of the pan. Place the English muffins over the bacon. Sprinkle the remaining bacon over the top.

In a mixing bowl, add the eggs, milk, onion powder and paprika. Whisk until combined and pour over the top of the casserole. Cover the pan with aluminum foil. Refrigerate at least 8 hours but not longer than 12 hours.

Remove the casserole from the refrigerator and let sit at room temperature for 30 minutes. Preheat the oven to 375°. Bake for 35 minutes. Remove the aluminum foil from the pan. Bake for 15 minutes or until a knife inserted in the center of the casserole comes out clean. Remove from the oven and cool for 5 minutes before serving.

While the casserole bakes, make the sauce. In the top of a double boiler, add the egg yolks, heavy cream, lemon juice and Dijon mustard. Whisk constantly and cook about 8 minutes or until the sauce thickens and coats the back of a spoon.

While constantly whisking, slowly drizzle in the melted butter. When all the butter is used and combined in the sauce, remove the pan from the heat. Spoon the sauce over individual servings of the casserole.

Italian Breakfast Strata

Makes 6 servings

1 lb. ground pork sausage
3 cups shredded mozzarella cheese
1/2 cup crumbled goat cheese
1/2 cup shredded Parmesan cheese
3 beaten eggs
1/2 cup ricotta cheese
1/4 cup whipping cream
1 tomato, cut into 6 slices
2 tbs. pesto sauce

In a skillet over medium heat, add the sausage. Stir frequently to break the sausage into crumbles as it cooks. Cook for 8 minutes or until the sausage is well browned and no longer pink. Remove the skillet from the heat and drain off any excess grease.

In a mixing bowl, add the sausage, 2 cups mozzarella cheese, goat cheese, Parmesan cheese, eggs, ricotta cheese and whipping cream. Whisk until combined. Spray a 11 x 7 baking dish with non stick cooking spray. Spoon the strata into the baking dish. Place the tomato slices over the top. Spread the pesto over the tomatoes.

Bake for 25 minutes. Sprinkle 1 cup mozzarella cheese over the top of the dish. Bake for 5-10 minutes or until the center of the strata is set. Remove the dish from the oven and serve. This is also a great dish for lunch or dinner.

Gruyere & Prosciutto Strata

Makes 9 servings

2 tbs. vegetable oil
4 oz. thinly sliced prosciutto, chopped
4 cups chopped onion
4 beaten eggs
2 1/2 cups whole milk
1/4 tsp. ground mustard
1/8 tsp. black pepper
8 cups cubed French bread
1 1/2 cups shredded Gruyere cheese

In a large skillet over medium high heat, add the vegetable oil. When the oil is hot, add the prosciutto. Saute for 4 minutes or until the prosciutto is crisp. Remove the prosciutto from the skillet and drain on paper towels. Add the onions to the skillet. Saute for 10 minutes or until the onions are tender. Remove the skillet from the heat.

In a mixing bowl, add the eggs, milk, ground mustard and black pepper. Whisk until combined. Reserve 2 tablespoons prosciutto and place in a small bowl in the refrigerator. Add the remaining prosciutto, onions and French bread to the eggs. Stir until combined.

Spray a 9 x 13 baking pan with non stick cooking spray. Spread half the egg mixture in the bottom of the pan. Sprinkle 3/4 cup Gruyere cheese over the mixture. Spread the remaining egg mixture over the cheese. Sprinkle 3/4 cup Gruyere cheese over the top. Cover the pan with plastic wrap. Refrigerate at least 8 hours but not longer than 12 hours.

Remove the strata from the refrigerator and let sit for 30 minutes at room temperature. Remove the plastic wrap from the pan. Preheat the oven to 350°. Bake for 20 minutes. Sprinkle the reserved 2 tablespoons prosciutto over the top of the strata. Bake for 15-20 minutes or until a knife inserted in the center of the strata comes out clean. Remove from the oven and cool for 5 minutes before serving.

Basic Breakfast Strata

Use any meat or cheese you desire. Italian sausage, pork sausage, chorizo, ground beef, bacon and ham are all good in this strata. Substitute your favorite bread if desired.

Makes 12 servings

1 lb. loaf Italian cheese bread, cubed
1 lb. your favorite ground meat, cooked
1 cup chopped green bell pepper
1 cup chopped onion
1 cup shredded cheese, use your favorite
6 eggs
2 cups whole milk
1 tsp. ground mustard

Spray a 9 x 13 baking pan with non stick cooking spray. Place the bread in the bottom of the baking pan. Spoon the meat, green bell pepper and onion over the bread. Sprinkle the cheese over the bread.

In a mixing bowl, add the eggs, milk and ground mustard. Whisk until combined and pour over the bread. Using a spatula, lightly press the bread to make sure the bread is coated in the eggs. Cover the baking pan with plastic wrap. Refrigerate for 8 hours but not more than 12 hours.

Remove the strata from the refrigerator. Let the strata sit for 30 minutes at room temperature. Preheat the oven to 350°. Remove the plastic wrap from the baking pan. Bake for 30 minutes or until a knife inserted in the center of the strata comes out clean. Remove from the oven and cool for 5 minutes before cutting.

Goat Cheese, Artichokes & Ham Strata

Makes 8 servings

2 cups whole milk
2 tbs. olive oil
1 lb. loaf sourdough bread, cut into 1" cubes
5 eggs
1 1/2 cups half and half cream
1 tbs. minced garlic
1 1/2 tsp. herbes de Provence
3/4 tsp. black pepper
1/2 tsp. ground nutmeg
1/2 tsp. crushed dried sage
1/2 tsp. crushed dried oregano
8 oz. crumbled goat cheese
12 oz. smoked cooked ham, chopped
3 jars marinated artichoke hearts, 6 oz. size
1 1/2 cups shredded Parmesan cheese
1 cup shredded fontina cheese

Spray a 9 x 13 baking pan with non stick cooking spray. In a large mixing bowl, add the milk and olive oil. Whisk until combined. Add the bread cubes to the bowl. Toss until the bread cubes are coated in the liquids. Let the bread sit for 10 minutes.

In a separate mixing bowl, add the eggs, half and half cream, garlic, herbes de Provence, black pepper, nutmeg, sage and oregano. Whisk until combined. Add the goat cheese and stir until combined.

Spread half the bread cubes in the baking pan. Sprinkle half the ham over the bread cubes. Drain the artichokes and cut in half lengthwise. Spread half the artichokes over the bread. Sprinkle 3/4 cup Parmesan cheese and 1/2 cup fontina cheese over the top. Repeat the layering steps using the remaining bread cubes, ham, artichokes, Parmesan and fontina cheese. Pour the eggs over the top. Do not stir. Cover the pan with plastic wrap. Refrigerate at least 2 hours but not longer than 12 hours.

Remove the pan from the refrigerator and remove the plastic wrap. Preheat the oven to 350°. Bake for 1 hour or until the center of the strata is set and the edges browned. Remove from the oven and let sit for 10 minutes before serving.

Creamy Egg Strata

Makes 8 servings

5 cups cubed French bread
6 tbs. unsalted butter, melted
2 cups shredded Swiss cheese
1/2 cup freshly grated Parmesan cheese
1/3 cup chopped onion
1 tsp. minced garlic
3 tbs. all purpose flour
1 1/2 cups chicken broth
3/4 cup dry white wine
1/2 tsp. salt
1/2 tsp. black pepper
1/4 tsp. ground nutmeg
1/2 cup sour cream
8 beaten eggs
2 tbs. minced fresh chives

Spray a 9 x 13 baking pan with non stick cooking spray. Add the bread cubes to the baking pan. Drizzle 3 tablespoons melted butter over the bread cubes. Sprinkle the Swiss & Parmesan cheeses over the bread.

In a sauce pan over medium heat, add 3 tablespoons melted butter, onion and garlic. Saute for 3 minutes. Add the all purpose flour to the pan. Stir constantly and cook for 2 minutes or until the flour begins to brown. While constantly whisking, add the chicken broth, white wine, salt, black pepper and nutmeg. Whisk constantly and cook about 5 minutes or until the sauce thickens and bubbles. Remove the pan from the heat and stir in the sour cream.

Add the eggs to a mixing bowl. While constantly whisking, slowly add 1/4 cup sauce to the eggs. Whisk until combined. Repeat this step one more time. Add the remaining sauce to the eggs and whisk until combined. Pour over the top of the strata. Cover the baking pan with plastic wrap. Refrigerate at least 8 hours but not more than 24 hours.

Remove the strata from the refrigerator and remove the plastic wrap. Let the strata sit for 30 minutes at room temperature. Preheat the oven to 350°. Bake for 30 minutes or until a knife inserted in the center of the strata comes out clean. Remove from the oven and sprinkle the chives over the top.

Four Cheese Zucchini Strata

Makes 8 servings

2 tbs. olive oil
5 cups diced zucchini
8 cups Italian garlic bread, cut into bite size pieces
1 cup shredded provolone cheese
1 cup shredded white cheddar cheese
1/2 cup crumbled blue cheese
1/2 cup grated Parmesan cheese
7 beaten eggs
2 cups whole milk
2 tbs. minced fresh parsley
1/2 tsp. salt
1/2 tsp. black pepper

In a skillet over medium heat, add the olive oil. When the oil is hot, add the zucchini. Saute for 5 minutes or until the zucchini is browned. Remove the skillet from the heat. Spray a 9 x 13 baking pan with non stick cooking spray.

Spread 4 cups bread pieces in the bottom of the pan. Sprinkle half the zucchini over the bread. Sprinkle 1/2 cup provolone cheese, 1/2 cup white cheddar cheese, 1/4 cup blue cheese and 1/4 cup Parmesan cheese over the bread. Repeat the layering step one more time.

In a mixing bowl, add the eggs, milk, parsley, salt and black pepper. Whisk until combined and pour over the top of the bread. Do not stir. Cover the pan with plastic wrap. Refrigerate at least 2 hours but not longer than 8 hours. Remove the pan from the refrigerator and remove the plastic wrap.

Preheat the oven to 350°. Bake for 45 minutes or until a knife inserted in the center of the strata comes out clean and the eggs are set. Remove from the oven and cool for 5 minutes before serving.

Mini Ham & Cheese Stratas

Makes 1 dozen

1/2 cup chopped onion
1 tsp. vegetable oil
5 eggs
1 1/2 cups whole milk
1 cup shredded cheddar cheese
2 tsp. Dijon mustard
1/4 tsp. salt
1/8 tsp. black pepper
3 cups day old Italian bread, cubed
1 cup cubed cooked ham
1 plum tomato, seeded & chopped

Preheat the oven to 350°. Spray a 12 cup muffin tin with non stick cooking spray. In a skillet over medium heat, add the onion and vegetable oil. Saute for 5 minutes. Remove the skillet from the heat and add the onion to a mixing bowl.

Add the eggs, milk, cheddar cheese, Dijon mustard, salt, black pepper, Italian bread, ham and tomato to the mixing bowl. Stir until combined. Spoon into the muffin cups. Bake for 20-25 minutes or until a toothpick inserted in the center of the stratas comes out clean. Remove from the oven and serve.

Ham & Broccoli Strata

Makes 8 servings

12 slices bread, crust removed
10 oz. pkg. frozen chopped broccoli, thawed & drained
2 cups diced cooked ham
6 beaten eggs
3 1/4 cups whole milk
1 tbs. dried minced onion
1/4 tsp. ground mustard
3 cups shredded sharp cheddar cheese

Cut the bread into small cubes. Spray a 9 x 13 baking pan with non stick cooking spray. Add the bread cubes, broccoli and ham to the baking pan. Stir until combined. In a mixing bowl, add the eggs, milk, minced onion, ground mustard and cheddar cheese. Whisk until combined and pour over the bread cubes. Do not stir. Cover the baking pan with plastic wrap. Refrigerate for 8 hours.

Remove the baking pan from the refrigerator. Let the strata sit for 30 minutes at room temperature. Remove the plastic wrap and discard. Preheat the oven to 325°. Bake for 50 minutes or until a toothpick inserted in the center of the dish comes out clean. Remove the pan from the oven and serve.

Ham Vegetable Strata

Makes 12 servings

1 small zucchini, cut into 1/2" slices
2 cups fresh broccoli florets
1/2 cup shredded carrot
12 slices bread, crust removed
1 cup cubed cooked ham
8 oz. can sliced mushrooms, drained
1 cup shredded sharp cheddar cheese
1 cup shredded Swiss cheese
12 eggs
2 1/2 cups whole milk
1/4 cup chopped onion
1/2 tsp. ground mustard
1/4 tsp. salt
1/8 tsp. black pepper
1 1/2 cups crushed cornflakes
1/4 cup melted unsalted butter

Add 1" of water to a sauce pan over medium heat. Add the zucchini, broccoli and carrot to the pan. Bring to a boil and place a lid on the pan. Cook for 5-6 minutes or until the vegetables are tender. Remove the pan from the heat and drain all the water from the pan.

Cut each bread slice in half. Spray a 9 x 13 baking pan with non stick cooking spray. Place half the bread slices in the bottom of the pan. Spoon half the cooked vegetables, 1/2 cup ham, half the mushrooms, 1/2 cup cheddar cheese and 1/2 cup Swiss cheese over the bread. Place the remaining bread slices over the top. Spoon the remaining vegetables, ham, mushrooms, cheddar cheese and Swiss cheese over the bread.

In a mixing bowl, add the eggs, milk, onion, ground mustard, salt and black pepper. Whisk until combined and pour over the top of the casserole. Do not stir. Cover the pan with plastic wrap. Refrigerate at least 8 hours but not more than 12 hours.

Remove the pan from the refrigerator and let sit at room temperature for 30 minutes. Preheat the oven to 350°. Remove the plastic wrap from the pan. Sprinkle the cornflakes over the top. Drizzle the melted butter over the cornflakes.

Bake for 45-50 minutes or until a knife inserted in the center of the strata comes out clean. Remove from the oven and cool for 5 minutes before serving.

Overnight Cheesy Vegetable Strata

Makes 8-10 servings

5 cups whole grain bread, cubed
2 cups chopped cooked broccoli
1 cup chopped cooked mushrooms
1/2 cup sliced green onions
1 1/4 cups shredded Swiss cheese
8 eggs
2 cups whole milk
1 tbs. Dijon mustard
1/2 tsp. black pepper
1/4 tsp. salt

Spray a 9 x 13 baking pan with non stick cooking spray. Spread the bread cubes, broccoli, mushrooms and green onions in the baking pan. Sprinkle 3/4 cup Swiss cheese over the top.

In a mixing bowl, add the eggs, milk, Dijon mustard, black pepper and salt. Whisk until combined and pour over the top of the casserole. Do not stir. Cover the pan with plastic wrap. Refrigerate for 8 hours but not more than 12 hours.

Preheat the oven to 350°. Remove the pan from the refrigerator and remove the plastic wrap. Bake for 30 minutes. Sprinkle 1/2 cup Swiss cheese over the top of the casserole. Bake for 10-12 minutes or until the casserole is set in the center and the cheese melted. Remove from the oven and cool for 5 minutes before serving.

Slow Cooker Egg & Broccoli Casserole

Makes 6 servings

24 oz. carton cottage cheese
10 oz. pkg. frozen chopped broccoli, thawed & drained
2 cups shredded cheddar cheese
6 beaten eggs
1/3 cup all purpose flour
1/4 cup melted unsalted butter
3 tbs. finely chopped onion
1/2 tsp. salt

Spray a 4 quart slow cooker with non stick cooking spray. Add all the ingredients to the slow cooker. Whisk until combined. Set the temperature to low. Cook for 2 1/2 - 3 hours or until the eggs are set and a meat thermometer reads at least 160°. Serve immediately.

Sun Dried Tomato & Spinach Egg Casserole

Makes 4 servings

4 cups frozen shredded hashbrowns, thawed
1 cup shredded cheddar cheese
1 cup frozen cut spinach, thawed & drained
1/4 cup sliced sun dried tomatoes in oil, drained
1 cup shredded mozzarella cheese
4 eggs
3/4 cup whole milk
1/4 tsp. salt
1/8 tsp. black pepper
2 tbs. shredded Parmesan cheese

In a mixing bowl, add the hashbrowns and cheddar cheese. Toss until combined. Preheat the oven to 350°. Spray an 8" square baking pan with non stick cooking spray. Spread half the hashbrowns in the bottom of the pan.

Spread the spinach and tomatoes over the hashbrowns. Spread the remaining hashbrowns over the spinach and tomatoes. Sprinkle the mozzarella cheese over the hashbrowns.

In a mixing bowl, add the eggs, milk, salt and black pepper. Whisk until combined and pour over the hashbrowns. Do not stir. Cover the pan with a lid or aluminum foil.

Bake for 30 minutes. Remove the aluminum foil from the pan. Sprinkle the Parmesan cheese over the top. Bake for 15 minutes or until a knife inserted in the center of the casserole comes out clean. The eggs should be set in the center when ready. Remove from the oven and serve.

Egg & Vegetable Casserole

Makes 6 servings

4 tbs. unsalted butter, melted
1 1/2 cups frozen hashbrowns
1 1/2 cups sliced fresh mushrooms
1/2 cup sliced green onion
10 oz. pkg. cut asparagus, thawed & drained
1/4 cup jarred roasted red bell peppers, drained & thinly sliced
6 eggs
1/2 cup half and half
1/2 tsp. lemon juice
1/4 tsp. salt
1/4 tsp. dried marjoram
1 cup soft breadcrumbs
1/4 cup shredded Parmesan cheese

Spray an 8" square baking pan with non stick cooking spray. Preheat the oven to 350°. In a large skillet over medium heat, add 2 tablespoons butter. When the butter is hot, add the hashbrowns, mushrooms and green onions. Saute for 6 minutes or until the hashbrowns are tender. Add the asparagus and roasted red bell peppers to the skillet. Stir until combined and remove the skillet from the heat.

Spoon the vegetables into the baking pan. In a mixing bowl, add the eggs, half and half, lemon juice, salt and marjoram. Stir until combined and pour over the vegetables. In small bowl, add the breadcrumbs, Parmesan cheese and 2 tablespoons butter. Stir until combined and sprinkle over the top of the casserole.

Bake for 10-12 minutes or until the center of the casserole is set and golden brown. Remove from the oven and serve.

Cheddar Vegetable Strata

This dish also makes a great lunch or dinner. Serve with a green salad for a hearty meal.

Makes 6 servings

4 cups cubed bread
2 cups frozen green beans, carrots & cauliflower blend, thawed & drained
1/3 cup sliced green onion
1 cup shredded cheddar cheese
4 eggs
1 cup whole milk
1/2 tsp. salt
1/2 tsp. dried marjoram
1/4 tsp. dry mustard
1/8 tsp. black pepper

Preheat the oven to 350°. Spray an 8" square baking pan with non stick cooking spray. Spread half the bread cubes in the pan. Spoon the vegetables over the bread. Sprinkle the green onions and cheddar cheese over the vegetables. Spread the remaining bread cubes over the top.

In a mixing bowl, add the eggs, milk, salt, marjoram, dry mustard and black pepper. Whisk until combined and pour over the bread and vegetables. Do not stir. Let the strata sit at room temperature for 15 minutes. Press the bread down in the liquid to make sure the bread is coated in the eggs.

Bake for 35 minutes or until a knife inserted in the center of the strata comes out clean. Remove from the oven and cool for 5 minutes before serving.

Mushroom Strata

Makes 4-6 servings

4 eggs
2 cups whole milk
2 tbs. melted unsalted butter
1 tsp. dry mustard
1/2 tsp. salt
2 cups fresh bread cubes
2 cups shredded cheddar cheese
1 cup cooked sliced mushrooms

In a mixing bowl, add the eggs. Whisk until combined. Add the milk, butter, dry mustard and salt to the eggs. Stir until combined. Add the bread cubes, cheddar cheese and mushrooms to the bowl. Stir until combined.

Lightly spray a 12 x 8 casserole dish with non stick cooking spray. Spoon the eggs into the casserole dish. Cover the dish with plastic wrap. Refrigerate at least 8 hours but not longer than 10 hours.

Remove the dish from the refrigerator and remove the plastic wrap. Preheat the oven to 350°. Bake for 50 minutes or until the center of the strata is set. Remove from the oven and serve.

Vegetable Egg Casserole

Makes 4 servings

6 beaten eggs
Salt and black pepper to taste
1 tbs. plain dry breadcrumbs
2 cups frozen stir fry vegetables
1 cup shredded cheddar cheese

I like to use a frozen broccoli, carrots, water chestnuts and red pepper blend for this recipe. Use your favorite frozen vegetable combinations.

Preheat the oven to 350°. Spray a non stick skillet with non stick cooking spray. Place the skillet over medium heat. Add the eggs to the skillet. Season to taste with salt and black pepper. Stir constantly and cook about 4 minutes or until the eggs are scrambled but still moist. Remove the skillet from the heat.

Spoon the eggs into a 1 1/2 quart casserole dish. Sprinkle the breadcrumbs over the eggs. Add the vegetables to a microwavable bowl. Microwave for 5 minutes or until the vegetables are tender. Drain off any liquid. Pat the vegetables dry if they are too moist. Spoon the vegetables over the eggs. Season to taste with salt and black pepper. Sprinkle the cheddar cheese over the top. Bake for 10 minutes or until the dish is hot and the cheese bubbly. Remove from the oven and serve.

Breakfast Crostatas

Makes 4 servings

8 oz. loaf unsliced French bread
1 tsp. dried basil
1/4 tsp. dried rosemary
1 1/2 cups diced cooked ham
1 1/2 cups shredded cheddar cheese
4 eggs
Salt and black pepper to taste

Cut the French bread in half lengthwise and then cut each half crosswise to form 4 squares. Press the bread down in the center so the crust acts as sides for the filling. Spray a baking sheet with non stick cooking spray. Place the bread on the baking sheet.

Sprinkle the basil, rosemary, ham and cheddar cheese over the bread. Press the ingredients down with a spatula. Make a well in the center of each bread square. Break an egg into each center. Sprinkle salt and black pepper to taste over the eggs.

Preheat the oven to 350°. Bake for 20 minutes or until the eggs are set. Remove the pan from the oven and serve.

Egg & Green Chile Rice Casserole

Makes 4 servings

3/4 cup dry instant brown rice, hot & cooked
1/2 cup chopped green onions
1/2 tsp. ground cumin
4 oz. can diced green chiles, drained
1/8 tsp. salt
4 beaten eggs
1/2 cup shredded cheddar cheese
1/4 cup pico de gallo
1 lime, quartered

Preheat the oven to 350°. Spray an 8" square baking pan with non stick cooking spray. Add the rice, green onions and cumin to the baking pan. Stir until combined. Spread the green chiles over the top. Sprinkle the salt over the casserole.

In a small bowl, add the eggs. Whisk until combined and pour over the top of the casserole. Bake for 30 minutes or until the center of the casserole is set. Sprinkle the cheddar cheese over the top. Bake for 5 minutes. Remove from the oven and serve with the pico de gallo and lime wedges.

Spicy Brunch Lasagna

Makes 16 servings

1 1/2 lbs. ground spicy Italian sausage
24 oz. carton cottage cheese
1/2 cup finely chopped green onions
1/4 cup minced fresh chives
1/4 cup grated carrot
18 eggs
1/3 cup whole milk
1/2 tsp. salt
1/2 tsp. black pepper
2 tbs. unsalted butter
15 oz. jar Alfredo sauce
1 tsp. dried Italian seasoning
8 no boil lasagna noodles
4 cups frozen shredded hashbrowns, thawed
2 cups shredded mozzarella cheese

In a large skillet over medium heat, add the Italian sausage. Stir frequently to break the sausage into crumbles as it cooks. Cook for 10 minutes or until the sausage is well browned and no longer pink. Remove the skillet from the heat and drain off any grease.

In a mixing bowl, add the cottage cheese, green onions, chives and carrot. Stir until combined. In a mixing bowl, add the eggs, milk, salt and black pepper. Whisk until combined. Add the butter to a skillet over medium heat. When the butter melts, add the eggs. Stir frequently and cook until the eggs are set but still moist. Remove the skillet from the heat.

In a small bowl, add the Alfredo sauce and Italian seasoning. Stir until combined. Spread half the sauce in the bottom of a 9 x 13 baking pan. Place 4 noodles over the sauce. Break the noodles to fit if needed. Spread the remaining sauce over the noodles. Place 4 noodles over the sauce.

Spread half the cottage cheese mixture, half the hashbrowns, half the scrambled eggs and half the sausage over the noodles. Sprinkle 2 cups mozzarella cheese over the top. Repeat the layering step using the remaining cottage cheese mixture, hashbrowns, eggs, sausage and cheese.

Cover the pan with plastic wrap. Refrigerate at least 8 hours but no longer than 24 hours. Remove the lasagna from the refrigerator and let sit at room temperature for 30 minutes. Remove the plastic wrap. Cover the pan with aluminum foil.

Preheat the oven to 350°. Bake for 45 minutes. Remove the aluminum foil from the pan. Bake for 15-20 minutes or until the lasagna is hot and bubbly. Remove from the oven and cool for 5 minutes before serving.

Overnight Southwestern Egg Bake

Makes 12 servings

12 eggs
1/2 cup whole milk
11 oz. can Mexicorn, drained
10 soft corn tortillas, 6" size
1 cup shredded Monterey Jack cheese
2 cups salsa
1 cup sour cream
1 cup guacamole

Spray a 9 x 13 baking pan with non stick cooking spray. In a mixing bowl, add the eggs and milk. Whisk until combined. Add the corn and stir until combined. Place the corn tortillas in the bottom of the baking pan. The tortillas may overlap. Pour the eggs over the tortillas. Sprinkle the Monterey Jack cheese over the top.

Cover the pan with aluminum foil. Refrigerate at least 8 hours but not longer than 12 hours. Preheat the oven to 375°. Remove from the refrigerator and bake for 25-30 minutes or until the eggs are completely set. Remove from the oven and remove the aluminum foil. Spoon the salsa over the top of the casserole. Spoon dollops of the sour cream and guacamole over the top and serve.

Creamy Ham & Egg Casserole

Makes 6 servings

2 cooked baking potatoes, peeled & sliced
4 hard boiled eggs, peeled & chopped
1 cup diced cooked ham
1/2 tsp. salt
1/4 tsp. black pepper
1 egg
1 1/2 cups sour cream
1/4 cup dry breadcrumbs
1 tbs. unsalted butter, melted

Preheat the oven to 350°. Spray a 11 x 7 casserole dish with non stick cooking spray. In a mixing bowl, add the potatoes, hard boiled eggs, ham, salt and black pepper. Toss until combined. In a small bowl, add the egg and sour cream. Whisk until combined and add to the potatoes. Toss until combined and spoon into the casserole dish.

Sprinkle the breadcrumbs over the top of the casserole. Drizzle the butter over the breadcrumbs. Bake for 25 minutes or until the casserole is hot and bubbly. Remove from the oven and serve.

Sausage, Egg & Chile Casserole

Makes 8 servings

1 lb. ground pork sausage
1 cup chopped celery
1/4 cup chopped onion
1/2 cup chopped green bell pepper
4 oz. can diced green chiles, drained
4 cups sandwich bread, cubed
4 eggs
3 cups whole milk
10.75 oz. can cream of mushroom soup
3 cups shredded cheddar cheese

In a skillet over medium heat, add the sausage. Stir frequently to break the sausage into crumbles as it cooks. Cook for 8 minutes or until the sausage is well browned and no longer pink. Drain off the excess grease.

Add the celery, onion and green bell pepper to the skillet. Saute for 5 minutes. Add the green chiles to the skillet. Stir until combined and remove the skillet from the heat.

Spray a 9 x 13 baking pan with non stick cooking spray. Spread half the bread cubes in the baking pan. Spread the sausage over the bread. Spread the remaining bread cubes over the top.

In a mixing bowl, add the eggs and milk. Whisk until combined and pour over the top of the casserole. Do not stir. Spread the cream of mushroom soup over the top. Preheat the oven to 350°. Bake for 45 minutes. Sprinkle the cheddar cheese over the casserole. Bake for 15 minutes. Remove from the oven and cool for 5 minutes before serving.

Southwest Biscuit Brunch Casserole

Makes 12 servings

2 tbs. unsalted butter
2 1/2 tbs. all purpose flour
2 cups whole milk
2 1/2 cups shredded sharp cheddar cheese
4 oz. can diced green chiles, drained
1/2 tsp. salt
1/4 tsp. black pepper
1 lb. ground pork sausage
1/4 cup chopped onion
13 eggs, beaten
2 cups self rising flour
1/3 cup vegetable oil
1/3 cup evaporated milk
2 tbs. chopped fresh cilantro

In a sauce pan over medium low heat, add the butter. When the butter melts, add the all purpose flour. Stir constantly and cook for 1 minute. Increase the heat to medium and add the milk. Stir constantly and cook until the sauce begins to thicken. Remove the pan from the heat and stir in 1 cup cheddar cheese, green chiles, salt and black pepper. Stir until the cheese melts. Keep the sauce warm while you prepare the casserole.

In a skillet over medium heat, add the sausage and onion. Stir frequently to break the sausage into crumbles as it cooks. Cook for 8 minutes or until the sausage is well browned and no longer pink. Drain off any excess grease.

Reduce the heat to low. Add 12 eggs to the skillet. Stir constantly and cook until the eggs are set but still moist. Remove the skillet from the heat and stir in the cheese sauce.

Preheat the oven to 400°. Spray a 9 x 13 baking pan with non stick cooking spray. Spoon the sausage mixture into the baking pan. In a mixing bowl, add the self rising flour, vegetable oil, 1 egg and evaporated milk. Stir until combined and a soft dough forms.

Lightly flour your work surface. Place the dough on the surface and knead 4 times. Roll the dough into a 12" square. Sprinkle 1 1/2 cups cheddar cheese over the dough. Roll the dough up like a jelly roll. With a sharp knife, cut the dough into twelve 1" slices. Place the slices over the top of the casserole. Bake for 25 minutes or until the biscuit slices are golden brown. Remove from the oven and sprinkle the cilantro over the top.

Breakfast Stuffing Casserole

Makes 8 servings

1 lb. ground pork sausage
1 tsp. dried Italian seasoning
1/2 tsp. salt
6 eggs
1/2 cup dry Cream of Wheat hot cereal
1 tsp. Tabasco sauce
4 cups cubed bread stuffing
2 cups shredded cheddar cheese

In a skillet over medium heat, add the sausage, Italian seasoning and salt. Stir frequently to break the sausage into crumbles as it cooks. Cook for 8 minutes or until the sausage is well browned and no longer pink. Remove the skillet from the heat and drain off the excess grease.

In a mixing bowl, add the eggs, Cream of Wheat cereal and Tabasco sauce. Whisk until combined. Add the bread stuffing and sausage to the bowl. Toss until the bread cubes are coated in the eggs. Spray a 9 x 13 baking pan with non stick cooking spray. Spoon the stuffing into the baking pan. Cover the pan with plastic wrap. Refrigerate at least 4 hours but not longer than 12 hours.

Preheat the oven to 350°. Remove the casserole from the refrigerator and remove the plastic wrap. Sprinkle the cheddar cheese over the top. Cover the pan with aluminum foil. Bake for 30 minutes. Remove the aluminum foil from the pan. Bake for 15 minutes or until the casserole is set in the center and lightly browned. Remove from the oven and cool for 5 minutes before serving.

Roasted Pepper & Sourdough Brunch Casserole

Makes 8 servings

3 cups sourdough bread cubes
12 oz. jar roasted red bell peppers, thinly sliced & drained
1 cup shredded sharp cheddar cheese
1 cup shredded Monterey Jack cheese
1 cup cottage cheese
6 eggs
1 cup whole milk
1/4 cup chopped fresh cilantro
1/4 tsp. black pepper

Spray a 11 x 7 casserole dish with non stick cooking spray. Place the bread cubes in the casserole dish. Place the roasted red bell peppers over the bread. Sprinkle the cheddar and Monterey Jack cheese over the top.

Add the cottage cheese to a food processor. Pulse until smooth. Add the eggs and milk to the food processor. Pulse until combined and pour over the bread in the casserole dish. Sprinkle the cilantro and black pepper over the top.

Cover the casserole dish with plastic wrap. Refrigerate at least 4 hours but not longer than 12 hours. Remove the dish from the refrigerator. Preheat the oven to 375°. Remove the plastic wrap from the dish. Bake for 40 minutes or until a knife inserted in the center of the casserole comes out clean and the casserole is golden brown. Remove from the oven and cool for 5 minutes before serving.

Mexican Breakfast Casserole

Makes 6 servings

1 lb. ground pork sausage
1/2 cup chopped onion
2 jalapeno peppers, seeded and chopped
6 bread slices, crust removed
3 cups shredded sharp cheddar cheese
6 eggs
2 cups whole milk
1 tsp. black pepper
1/2 tsp. salt
1 cup salsa

In a large skillet over medium heat, add the sausage, onion and jalapeno peppers. Stir frequently to break the sausage into crumbles as it cooks. Cook for 8 minutes or until the sausage is well browned and no longer pink. Remove the skillet from the heat and drain off any excess grease.

Lightly spray a 11 x 7 baking dish with non stick cooking spray. Place the bread slices in the baking dish. Spoon the sausage and 1 cup cheddar cheese over the bread.

In a mixing bowl, add the eggs, milk, black pepper and salt. Whisk until combined and pour over the bread slices. Sprinkle 2 cups cheddar cheese over the top. Cover the dish with aluminum foil. Refrigerate at least 8 hours but not more than 24 hours before baking.

Preheat the oven to 350°. Remove the dish from the refrigerator and remove the aluminum foil. Bake for 45 minutes or until the casserole is set in the center. Remove the dish from the oven and cool for 5 minutes before serving. Spoon the salsa over the top and serve.

Sausage Ham Breakfast Casserole

Makes 4 servings

8 oz. ground hot pork sausage
3 slices white bread
2 cups shredded sharp cheddar cheese
3 eggs
1 cup whole milk
1 tsp. yellow prepared mustard
1/4 tsp. black peppcr
2 cups chopped cooked ham

In a skillet over medium heat, add the sausage. Stir frequently to break the sausage into crumbles as it cooks. Cook for 6 minutes or until the sausage is well browned and no longer pink. Remove the skillet from the heat and drain off any excess grease.

Lightly spray an 8" square baking pan with non stick cooking spray. Place the bread slices in the baking pan. Spoon the sausage over the bread. Sprinkle 1 cup cheddar cheese over the sausage.

In a mixing bowl, add the eggs, milk, mustard and black pepper. Whisk until combined and pour over the bread. Sprinkle 1 cup cheddar cheese over the top. Sprinkle the ham over the top of the casserole. Cover the pan with aluminum foil. Refrigerate at least 2 hours but not more than 12 hours.

Preheat the oven to 350°. Do not remove the aluminum foil. Bake for 30 minutes. Remove the aluminum foil and bake for 15 minutes or until the casserole is set in the center. Remove the pan from the oven and cool for 15 minutes before serving.

Deluxe Breakfast Casserole

Makes 12 servings

6 oz. pkg. onion and garlic salad croutons
2 cups shredded cheddar cheese
1 1/2 cups diced cooked ham
4 eggs
2 3/4 cups whole milk
3/4 tsp. ground mustard
10.75 oz. can cream of mushroom soup
30 oz. pkg. shredded frozen hashbrowns, thawed
1/2 tsp. paprika
1/4 tsp. black pepper

Spray a 9 x 13 baking pan with non stick cooking spray. Spread the croutons in the bottom of the pan. Sprinkle the cheddar cheese and ham over the croutons. In a mixing bowl, add the eggs, 2 1/4 cups milk and ground mustard. Whisk until combined and pour over the top of the casserole. Cover the pan with plastic wrap. Refrigerate for 8 hours but not longer than 12 hours.

Remove the casserole from the refrigerator and let sit at room temperature for 30 minutes. Remove the plastic wrap from the pan. Preheat the oven to 350°. In a small bowl, add the cream of mushroom soup and 1/2 cup milk. Stir until combined and spread over the top of the casserole. Spread the hashbrowns over the soup. Sprinkle the paprika and black pepper over the hashbrowns.

Cover the pan with aluminum foil. Bake for 30 minutes. Remove the aluminum foil from the pan. Bake for 35 minutes or until the casserole is bubbly, set in the center and browned. Remove from the oven and serve.

Potato & Egg Dinner Casserole

Makes 4 servings

4 cups diced peeled potatoes
8 bacon slices, cooked & crumbled
4 hard boiled eggs, peeled & sliced
10.75 oz. can cream of mushroom soup
1/2 cup whole milk
1/2 cup chopped onion
1 tbs. chopped green bell pepper
1 tbs. chopped red bell pepper
1 cup shredded cheddar cheese

Spray a 2 quart baking dish with non stick cooking spray. Spread 2 cups potatoes in the bottom of the baking dish. Sprinkle the bacon over the potatoes. Place the hard boiled eggs over the potatoes. Place the remaining potatoes over the top.

In a sauce pan over medium heat, add the cream of mushroom soup, milk, onion, green bell pepper and red bell pepper. Stir until combined and bring to a boil. Remove the pan from the heat and spread over the potatoes. Sprinkle the cheddar cheese over the top.

Preheat the oven to 350°. Cover the baking dish with aluminum foil. Bake for 20 minutes. Remove the aluminum foil from the baking dish. Bake for 15 minutes or until the casserole is hot and bubbly. Remove from the oven and serve.

Eggs Florentine Casserole

Makes 12 servings

10 oz. pkg. frozen spinach, thawed
1 cup shredded cheddar cheese
1 lb. ground pork sausage
2 cups sliced fresh mushrooms
1 cup chopped green onion
2 tbs. melted unsalted butter
12 eggs, beaten
2 cups whipping cream
1 cup shredded Swiss cheese
1/4 tsp. paprika

Drain any liquid from the spinach. Spray a 9 x 13 baking pan with non stick cooking spray. Sprinkle the cheddar cheese in the bottom of the pan. Spread the spinach over the cheddar cheese.

In a skillet over medium heat, add the sausage. Stir frequently to break the sausage into crumbles as it cooks. Cook for 8 minutes or until the sausage is well browned and no longer pink. Remove the sausage from the skillet and spoon over the spinach.

Drain any excess grease from the skillet. Add the mushrooms, green onions and butter to the skillet. Saute for 5 minutes. Remove the skillet from the heat and spoon the mushrooms and green onions over the sausage.

In a mixing bowl, add the eggs and whipping cream. Whisk until combined and pour over the top of the casserole. Do not stir. Sprinkle the Swiss cheese and paprika over the top of the casserole.

Preheat the oven to 350°. Bake for 40 minutes or until the casserole is set in the center. Remove the casserole from the oven and cool for 5 minutes before serving.

Farmer's Omelet Casserole

Makes 12 servings

3 cups cubed hashbrown potatoes
1 cup chopped green bell pepper
1/3 cup chopped onion
1 tbs. vegetable oil
18 beaten eggs
2 1/3 cups chopped cooked ham
1 1/4 cups diced tomato
1/2 tsp. salt
1/2 tsp. black pepper
1 1/2 cups shredded Monterey Jack cheese

In a skillet over medium heat, add the potatoes, green bell pepper, onion and vegetable oil. Stir frequently and cook for 8 minutes or until the potatoes are browned. Remove the skillet from the heat and spoon the potatoes into a mixing bowl. Add the eggs, ham, tomato, salt and black pepper to the bowl. Whisk until combined.

Preheat the oven to 325°. Spray a 9 x 13 baking pan with non stick cooking spray. Spoon the filling into the baking pan. Bake for 40 minutes or until the casserole is set in the center and golden brown. Sprinkle the Monterey Jack cheese over the top. Bake for 5 minutes or until the cheese melts. Remove the casserole from the oven and serve.

Bacon, Egg & Potato Bake

Makes 8 servings

30 oz. pkg. cubed frozen hashbrowns, thawed
1 lb. bacon slices, cooked & crumbled
1 cup shredded cheddar cheese
1/4 tsp. salt
8 eggs
2 cups whole milk
Paprika to taste

Preheat the oven to 350°. Spray a 9 x 13 baking pan with non stick cooking spray. In a mixing bowl, add the hashbrowns, bacon, 1/2 cup cheddar cheese and salt. Stir until combined and spread in the bottom of the baking pan.

In a mixing bowl, add the eggs and milk. Whisk until combined and pour over the top of the hashbrowns. Do not stir. Sprinkle paprika to taste over the top. Bake for 45 minutes or until a knife inserted near the center of the casserole comes out clean. Remove from the oven and sprinkle 1/2 cup cheddar cheese over the top.

Spinach Breakfast Casserole

This casserole is also great for dinner or brunch.

Makes 8 servings

20 oz. pkg. refrigerated hashbrowns
1 tbs. olive oil
10 oz. pkg. frozen spinach, thawed and drained
4 oz. Swiss cheese, cubed
4 oz. thinly sliced cooked ham, chopped
8 eggs
1/2 cup whole milk
1 tbs. prepared basil pesto
1 cup Bisquick
1/4 tsp. salt
1/8 tsp. black pepper
1 1/2 cups shredded Asiago cheese
2 tbs. minced fresh basil

Spray a 9 x 13 baking pan with non stick cooking spray. Preheat the oven to 350°. In a mixing bowl, add the hashbrowns and olive oil. Toss until combined. Spread the hashbrowns in the bottom of the baking pan. Bake for 25 minutes or until the edges of the hashbrowns are golden brown. Remove the pan from the oven.

Spread the spinach over the hashbrowns. Sprinkle the Swiss cheese over the hashbrowns. Place the ham over the top. In a mixing bowl, add the eggs, milk, pesto, Bisquick, salt, black pepper and Asiago cheese. Whisk until combined and pour over the top of the casserole. Do not stir.

Bake for 25 minutes or until the center of the casserole is set. Remove the casserole from the oven and cool for 10 minutes before serving. Sprinkle the basil over the top and serve.

Italian Sausage Brunch Casserole

Makes 8 servings

1 lb. ground Italian sausage
1 cup chopped onion
7 oz. jar roasted red bell peppers, drained
10 oz. pkg. frozen chopped spinach, thawed & drained
1 cup all purpose flour
1/4 cup grated Parmesan cheese
1 tsp. dried basil
1/2 tsp. salt
2 cups whole milk
8 eggs
1 cup shredded provolone cheese

Preheat the oven to 425°. Spray a 9 x 13 baking pan with non stick cooking spray. In a skillet over medium heat, add the Italian sausage and onions. Stir frequently to break the sausage into crumbles as it cooks. Cook for 8 minutes or until the sausage is well browned and no longer pink. Remove the skillet from the heat and drain off the excess grease.

Spread the sausage in the bottom of the baking pan. Chop the red bell peppers and sprinkle half the peppers over the sausage. Spread the spinach over the sausage and peppers.

In a mixing bowl, add the all purpose flour, Parmesan cheese, basil, salt and milk. Whisk until smooth and combined. Add the eggs to the bowl. Whisk until combined and pour over the sausage and vegetables in the baking pan. Do not stir.

Bake for 20 minutes or until the center of the casserole is almost set. Sprinkle the provolone cheese over the top. Bake for 5 minutes or until the casserole is set in the center and the cheese melted. Remove from the oven and cool for 5 minutes before cutting.

Brunch Egg Bake

Makes 12 servings

3 cups shredded cheddar cheese
3 cups shredded mozzarella cheese
1 cup cooked sliced mushrooms
1/2 cup chopped red bell pepper
1/3 cup sliced green onion
2 tbs. unsalted butter
2 cups diced cooked ham
1/2 cup all purpose flour
1 3/4 cups whole milk
8 beaten eggs
2 tbs. minced fresh parsley
1/2 tsp. salt
1/2 tsp. dried basil
1/4 tsp. black pepper

Spray a 9 x 13 baking pan with non stick cooking spray. Add the cheddar and mozzarella cheeses to a mixing bowl. Toss until combined. Spread half the cheeses in the bottom of the baking pan. In a skillet over medium heat, add the mushrooms, red bell pepper, green onion and butter. Saute for 5 minutes. Remove the skillet from the heat. Spoon the vegetables over the cheeses.

Sprinkle the ham and remaining cheeses over the vegetables. In a mixing bowl, add the all purpose flour, milk, eggs, parsley, salt, basil and black pepper. Whisk until combined and pour over the top of the casserole. Do not stir.

Preheat the oven to 350°. Bake for 35 minutes or until a toothpick inserted in the center of the casserole comes out clean. Remove the casserole from the oven and serve.

Potato Huevos Rancheros Casserole

Makes 12 servings

32 oz. pkg. frozen tater tots
12 eggs
1 cup whole milk
1 1/2 tsp. crushed dried oregano
1 1/2 tsp. ground cumin
1/2 tsp. chili powder
1/4 tsp. garlic powder
2 cups shredded Mexican cheese blend
16 oz. jar thick & chunky salsa
1 cup sour cream
2 tbs. chopped fresh cilantro

Preheat the oven to 375°. Spray a 9 x 13 baking pan with non stick cooking spray. Place the tater tots in the baking pan. In a mixing bowl, add the eggs, milk, oregano, cumin, chili powder and garlic powder. Whisk until combined and pour over the tater tots.

Bake for 35 minutes or until a knife inserted near the center of the casserole comes out clean. Sprinkle the Mexican cheese blend over the casserole. Bake for 5 minutes or until the cheese melts and the casserole is set in the center. Remove from the oven. Cool for 5 minutes. Spread the salsa over the top. Spoon dollops of the sour cream over the casserole. Sprinkle the cilantro over the top and serve.

Cheesy Potato Bake With Eggs

Makes 8 servings

2 tbs. unsalted butter
1/2 cup finely chopped onion
4 tsp. all purpose flour
1 tsp. salt
3/4 tsp. black pepper
1 1/2 cups whole milk
2 cups shredded sharp cheddar cheese
3 lbs. russet potatoes, peeled & thinly sliced
1 tbs. vegetable oil
1 1/2 cups chopped fresh broccoli
8 eggs
2 tbs. water
6 bacon slices, cooked & crumbled
1 1/2 cups chopped tomato

Preheat the oven to 350°. In a sauce pan over medium heat, add the butter. When the butter melts, add the onion. Saute for 4 minutes. Add the all purpose flour, 1/2 teaspoon salt and 1/2 teaspoon black pepper. Stir constantly and cook for 1 minute. Add the milk to the pan. Stir constantly and cook until the sauce thickens. Remove the pan from the heat. Add the cheddar cheese to the pan. Stir until the cheese melts.

Spray a 9 x 13 baking pan with non stick cooking spray. Layer half the potatoes in the bottom of the pan. Spread half the cheese sauce over the potatoes. Layer the remaining potatoes over the cheese sauce. Spread the remaining cheese sauce over the top. Cover the pan with aluminum foil. Bake for 50 minutes or until the potatoes are tender.

In a skillet over medium heat, add the vegetable oil. When the oil is hot, add the broccoli. Saute for 5 minutes. In a mixing bowl, add the eggs and water. Whisk until combined and add to the skillet. Stir frequently and cook until the eggs are set and scrambled. Remove the skillet from the heat. Spread the eggs over the top of the potatoes. Sprinkle the bacon and tomato over the top.

Golden Egg Casserole

Makes 8 servings

2 tbs. unsalted butter
1 cup sliced fresh mushrooms
1 green bell pepper, chopped
10 eggs
1/2 cup all purpose flour
1 tsp. baking powder
1/4 tsp. salt
16 oz. container cottage cheese
2 cups shredded Monterey Jack cheese
8 oz. ground pork sausage, cooked and crumbled
6 bacon slices, cooked and crumbled
2 oz. can sliced black olives, drained

In a skillet over medium heat, add the butter, mushrooms and green bell pepper. Saute for 5 minutes or until the vegetables are tender. Remove the pan from the heat and cool for 10 minutes.

In a mixing bowl, add the eggs, all purpose flour, baking powder and salt. Whisk until combined. Add the vegetables from the skillet, cottage cheese, Monterey Jack cheese, sausage, bacon and olives to the bowl. Whisk until combined.

Preheat the oven to 400°. Spray a 9 x 13 baking pan with non stick cooking spray. Pour the casserole into the baking pan. Bake for 15 minutes. Reduce the oven temperature to 350°. Bake for 15 minutes or until the center of the casserole is set and lightly browned. Remove the casserole from the oven and serve.

Amish Breakfast Casserole

Makes 12 servings

1 lb. sliced bacon, diced
1 cup chopped onion
6 beaten eggs
4 cups frozen shredded hashbrowns, thawed
2 cups shredded cheddar cheese
1 1/2 cups cottage cheese
1 1/4 cups shredded Swiss cheese

Preheat the oven to 350°. In a large skillet over medium heat, add the bacon and onion. Cook for 8 minutes or until the bacon is crisp. Remove the skillet from the heat and drain off the excess grease. Add the bacon and onion to a large mixing bowl.

Add the eggs, hashbrowns, cheddar cheese, cottage cheese and Swiss cheese to the bowl. Stir until well combined. Spray a 9 x 13 baking pan with non stick cooking spray. Spoon the casserole into the baking pan. Bake for 35 minutes or until a knife inserted near the center of the casserole comes out clean. Remove from the oven and let the casserole sit for 10 minutes before serving.

Slow Cooker Breakfast Casserole

Makes 12 servings

30 oz. pkg. frozen shredded hashbrowns
1 lb. ground pork sausage, cooked
1 cup chopped onion
4 oz. can chopped green chiles, drained
1 1/2 cups shredded cheddar cheese
12 eggs
1 cup whole milk
1/2 tsp. salt
1/2 tsp. black pepper

In a mixing bowl, add the hashbrowns, sausage, onion, green chiles and cheddar cheese. Stir until combined. Spray a 5 quart slow cooker with non stick cooking spray. Spread the hashbrown mixture in the slow cooker.

In a mixing bowl, add the eggs, milk, salt and black pepper. Whisk until combined and pour over the ingredients in the slow cooker. Do not stir. Set the temperature to low. Cook for 7-8 hours or until a knife inserted in the center of the casserole comes out clean.

Sausage Mushroom Breakfast Casserole

Makes 12 servings

1 lb. ground pork sausage
2 cups sliced fresh mushrooms
6 cups cubed bread
2 cups shredded sharp cheddar cheese
1 cup chopped fresh tomatoes
10 beaten eggs
3 cups whole milk
2 tsp. ground mustard
1/2 tsp. salt
1/4 tsp. black pepper

In a skillet over medium heat, add the sausage and mushrooms. Stir frequently to break the sausage into crumbles as it cooks. Cook for 10 minutes or until the sausage is well browned and no longer pink. Remove the skillet from the heat and drain off the excess grease.

Spray a 9 x 13 baking pan with non stick cooking spray. Spread half the bread cubes in the baking pan. Spoon 2 cups sausage and mushrooms over the bread. Sprinkle 1 cup cheddar cheese and 1/2 cup tomatoes over the bread. Repeat the layering step one more time.

In a mixing bowl, add the eggs, milk, ground mustard, salt and black pepper. Whisk until combined and pour over the top of the casserole. Do not stir. Preheat the oven to 350°. Bake for 50 minutes or until the casserole is set in the center. Remove from the oven and cool for 5 minutes before serving.

Egg & Mushroom Bake

Makes 8 servings

2 tbs. unsalted butter
16 oz. pkg. sliced fresh mushrooms
2 green onions, chopped
2 tbs. melted unsalted butter
3 tbs. all purpose flour
3/4 tsp. salt
1/4 tsp. black pepper
1 cup whole milk
1/2 cup heavy whipping cream
1/2 cup plus 2 tbs. grated Parmesan cheese
16 eggs
1/4 cup unsalted butter, cubed

In a large oven proof skillet over medium heat, add 2 tablespoons butter. When the butter melts, add the mushrooms and 1 green onion. Saute for 7 minutes or until the mushrooms are tender. Remove from the heat. Remove the mushrooms and onions from the skillet and drain on paper towels. Wipe the skillet clean.

In a sauce pan over medium heat, add 2 tablespoons melted butter, all purpose flour, 1/4 teaspoon salt and 1/8 teaspoon black pepper. Stir constantly and cook for 2 minutes. Add the milk and heavy whipping cream to the pan. Stir constantly and cook until the sauce thickens. Add 2 tablespoons Parmesan cheese to the pan. Stir until the cheese melts and remove the pan from the heat.

In a mixing bowl, add the eggs, 1/2 teaspoon salt and 1/8 teaspoon black pepper. Whisk until combined. Add 1/4 cup butter to the skillet used to cook the mushrooms. When the butter melts, add the eggs. Stir occasionally and cook until the eggs thicken and are set. Remove the skillet from the heat.

Spread half the sauce over the eggs. Spoon the mushrooms and green onions over the top. Spread the remaining sauce over the top. Preheat the oven to the broiler position. Sprinkle 1/2 cup Parmesan cheese over the top. Broil for 5 minutes or until the top of the dish is lightly browned. Remove from the oven and sprinkle 1 green onion over the top.

Slow Cooker Ham & Eggs

Makes 6 servings

6 eggs
1 cup Bisquick
2/3 cup whole milk
1/3 cup sour cream
2 tbs. minced fresh parsley
2 garlic cloves, minced
1/2 tsp. salt
1/2 tsp. black pepper
1 cup cubed cooked ham
1 cup shredded Swiss cheese
1/2 cup finely chopped onion
1/3 cup grated Parmesan cheese

Spray a 4 quart slow cooker with non stick cooking spray. In a mixing bowl, add the eggs, Bisquick, milk, sour cream, parsley, garlic, salt and black pepper. Whisk until combined. Add the ham, Swiss cheese, onion and Parmesan cheese to the bowl. Whisk until combined.

Pour the casserole into the slow cooker. Set the temperature to low. Cook for 3-4 hours or until the eggs are set.

Sausage & Egg Squares

Makes 12 servings

8 ct. can refrigerated crescent rolls
1 lb. ground pork sausage
1/4 cup chopped onion
6 beaten eggs
2 tbs. chopped green bell pepper
1/2 tsp. dried oregano
1/2 tsp. black pepper
1/4 tsp. garlic salt
1 cup shredded mozzarella cheese

Preheat the oven to 375°. Spray a 9 x 13 baking pan with non stick cooking spray. Remove the crescent roll dough from the can. Pat the dough in the bottom of the baking pan. Press any perforations closed with your fingers. Bake for 6 minutes or until golden brown. Remove the pan from the oven.

While the crust cooks, add the sausage and onion to a skillet over medium heat. Stir frequently to break the sausage into crumbles as it cooks. Cook for 8 minutes or until the sausage is well browned and no longer pink. Remove the skillet from the heat and drain off the excess grease.

In a mixing bowl, add the eggs, green bell pepper, oregano, black pepper and garlic salt. Whisk until combined and pour over the crust. Spoon the sausage over the top. Bake for 15-20 minutes or until the eggs are set. Sprinkle the mozzarella cheese over the top. Bake for 5 minutes. Remove from the oven and cool for 5 minutes before serving.

Cinnamon Raisin Strata

Makes 4 servings

1/4 cup unsalted butter, softened
3 tbs. ground cinnamon
8 slices day old raisin bread
4 tbs. light brown sugar
6 eggs
1 1/2 cups whole milk
3 tbs. maple syrup
1 tsp. vanilla extract
Powdered sugar to taste

Spray an 8" square baking pan with non stick cooking spray. In a small bowl, add the butter and cinnamon. Stir until combined and spread on one side of each bread slice. Place 4 slices, buttered side up, in the baking pan. Cut the bread slices to fit if necessary. Sprinkle 2 tablespoons brown sugar over the bread. Repeat the layering step one more time.

In a mixing bowl, add the eggs, milk, maple syrup and vanilla extract. Whisk until combined and pour over the bread. Cover the pan with plastic wrap and refrigerate for 8 hours.

Preheat the oven to 350°. Remove the pan from the refrigerator. Bake for 35-40 minutes or until a knife inserted in the center of the strata comes out clean. Remove from the oven and cool for 5 minutes. Sprinkle powdered sugar to taste over the top and serve.

Cinnamon Apple French Toast Casserole

Makes 8 servings

1 lb. loaf French bread, cut into 1 1/2" slices
3 1/2 cups whole milk
9 eggs
1 1/2 cups granulated sugar
1 tbs. vanilla extract
1/2 tsp. salt
6 apples, peeled, cored & sliced
1 tsp. ground cinnamon
1/2 tsp. ground nutmeg
Powdered sugar to taste

Spray a 9 x 13 baking pan with non stick cooking spray. Place the bread slices in the baking pan. Do not overlap the slices. All the bread slices may not fit. Cut the bread slices if needed to fit.

In a mixing bowl, add the milk, eggs, 1 cup granulated sugar, vanilla extract and salt. Whisk until combined. Pour half the eggs over the bread. Place the apple slices over the top. Pour the remaining eggs over the apples. In a small bowl, add 1/2 cup granulated sugar, cinnamon and nutmeg. Stir until combined and sprinkle over the top of the casserole.

Cover the pan with plastic wrap. Refrigerate at least 8 hours but no longer than 12 hours. Remove from the refrigerator and remove the plastic wrap. Preheat the oven to 350°. Bake for 1 hour or until the casserole is set in the center and browned. Remove from the oven and cool for 5 minutes. Sprinkle powdered sugar to taste over the top of the casserole.

4 SANDWICHES & SALADS

Sandwiches are a delicious way to eat eggs. Fried or hard boiled eggs over greens are a nice change of pace. Of course, recipes for egg salad sandwich fillings are included.

Toasted Scrambled Egg Sandwiches

Makes 4 sandwiches

4 beaten eggs
1 tbs. whole milk
1/4 tsp. salt
1/4 tsp. black pepper
6 tbs. unsalted butter
8 bread slices, 1/2" thick
4 bacon slices, cooked
1/4 cup shredded cheddar cheese

In a small bowl, add the eggs, milk, salt and black pepper. Whisk until combined. In a skillet over medium heat, add 1 tablespoon butter. When the butter melts, add the eggs. Stir frequently and cook until the eggs are set and scrambled. Remove the skillet from the heat.

Spread the butter on one side of each bread slice. Place 4 bread slices, buttered side down, in a large skillet. Spoon the eggs over the bread. Place the bacon slices over the eggs. Sprinkle the cheddar cheese over the top. Place the remaining bread slices, buttered side up, over the sandwiches.

Place the skillet over medium heat. Cook for 3 minutes on each side or until golden brown. Remove from the heat and serve. You can cook the sandwiches on a panini press instead of using a skillet.

Ham, Egg & Cheese Breakfast Sandwich

Makes 2 sandwiches

1/4 cup chopped red bell pepper
2 tbs. sliced green onions
1/2 cup diced cooked ham
4 eggs
Salt and black pepper to taste
4 slices whole grain bread
2 oz. sliced cheddar cheese

Spray a skillet with non stick cooking spray. Place the skillet over medium heat. When the skillet is hot, add the red bell pepper. Saute for 3 minutes. Add the green onions and ham to the skillet. Saute for 3 minutes.

In a mixing bowl, add the eggs. Whisk until combined. Season to taste with salt and black pepper. Add the eggs to the skillet. Stir frequently and cook about 3 minutes or until the eggs are set. Remove the skillet from the heat.

Spray one side of each bread slice with non stick cooking spray. Place a grill pan over medium heat or use a panini press to cook the sandwiches. Place a cheese slice on the other side of each bread slice. Spoon the eggs over the cheese slices. Place the top bread slice, sprayed side up, over the eggs.

When the skillet is hot, add the sandwiches. Press down with a spatula. Cook for 3 minutes on each side or until the sandwiches are golden brown and the cheese melted. Remove from the heat and serve.

Bacon, Egg & Muenster Cheese Bagels

Makes 4 servings

4 bagels, split & toasted
1/2 cup garden vegetable cream cheese spread
1/2 cup sliced pimento stuffed olives
8 bacon strips, halved
4 large eggs
4 slices Muenster cheese

Spread each bagel half with the cream cheese spread. Place the olives over the cream cheese on the bottom pieces. In a skillet over medium heat, add the bacon. Cook for 5 minutes or until the bacon is crisp. Remove the bacon from the skillet and drain on paper towels.

Break the eggs into the skillet. Reduce the heat to low. Cook about 2 minutes or until the yolks are set but not hard. Remove the skillet from the heat. Place the bacon over the olives. Place a fried egg over the top. Place a slice of Muenster cheese over the eggs. Place the top bagels on the sandwiches and serve.

Scrambled Egg & Fontina Sandwiches

Makes 4 sandwiches

4 beaten eggs
1 tbs. whole milk
1/4 tsp. salt
1/4 tsp. black pepper
6 tbs. unsalted butter
8 bread slices, 1/2" thick
4 bacon slices, cooked
1 cup shredded fontina cheese

In a small bowl, add the eggs, milk, salt and black pepper. Whisk until combined. In a skillet over medium heat, add 1 tablespoon butter. When the butter melts, add the eggs. Stir frequently and cook until the eggs are set and scrambled. Remove the skillet from the heat.

Spread the remaining butter on one side of each bread slice. Place 4 bread slices, buttered side down, in a large skillet. Spoon the eggs over the bread. Place the bacon slices over the eggs. Sprinkle the fontina cheese over the top. Place the remaining bread slices, buttered side up, over the sandwiches.

Place the skillet over medium heat. Cook for 3 minutes on each side or until golden brown. Remove from the heat and serve. You can cook the sandwiches on a panini press instead of using a skillet.

Ham & Cheese Sauce Topped English Muffins

Makes 6 servings

1/3 cup all purpose flour
1/8 tsp. salt
1/8 tsp. black pepper
1 3/4 cups whole milk
4 oz. Velveeta cheese, cubed
1 1/2 cups chopped cooked ham
4 hard boiled eggs, chopped
1/2 cup mayonnaise
1/4 cup sliced green onions
1/4 cup chopped red pimentos
6 English muffins, split and toasted

In a sauce pan over medium heat, add the all purpose flour, salt, black pepper and milk. Stir constantly and cook until the sauce is smooth and begins to thicken. Add the Velveeta cheese to the pan. Stir until the cheese melts. Remove the pan from the heat.

Add the ham, eggs, mayonnaise, green onions and red pimentos to the pan. Stir until combined. Place the English muffins on serving plates. Spoon the sauce over the top and serve.

Wild Mushroom & Cheddar Sandwiches

Makes 4 sandwiches

4 beaten eggs
1 tbs. whole milk
1/4 tsp. salt
1/4 tsp. black pepper
6 tbs. unsalted butter
1 1/2 cups sliced mushrooms
8 bread slices, 1/2" thick
4 bacon slices, cooked
1/4 cup shredded cheddar cheese

In a small bowl, add the eggs, milk, salt and black pepper. Whisk until combined. In a skillet over medium heat, add 1 tablespoon butter. When the butter melts, add the mushrooms. Saute for 6 minutes. Add the eggs to the skillet. Stir frequently and cook until the eggs are set and scrambled. Remove the skillet from the heat.

Spread the remaining butter on one side of each bread slice. Place 4 bread slices, buttered side down, in a large skillet. Spoon the eggs over the bread. Place the bacon slices over the eggs. Sprinkle the cheddar cheese over the top. Place the remaining bread slices, buttered side up, over the sandwiches.

Place the skillet over medium heat. Cook for 3 minutes on each side or until golden brown. Remove from the heat and serve. Use tomato slices in place of the bacon for a lighter sandwich if desired. You can cook the sandwiches on a panini press instead of using a skillet.

Grilled Bacon & Egg Biscuit

Makes 4 servings

4 beaten eggs
1 tbs. whole milk
1/4 tsp. salt
1/4 tsp. black pepper
6 tbs. unsalted butter, softened
4 hot cooked biscuits, split
4 bacon slices, cooked & halved
1/4 cup shredded cheddar cheese

In a small bowl, add the eggs, milk, salt and black pepper. Whisk until combined. In a skillet over medium heat, add 1 tablespoon butter. When the butter melts, add the eggs. Stir frequently and cook for 3-4 minutes or until the eggs are set. Remove the skillet from the heat.

Spread the remaining butter on the outside top and bottom of each biscuit. Place the eggs on the bottom biscuits. Place the bacon over the eggs. Sprinkle the cheddar cheese over the top. Place the biscuit tops on the sandwiches.

In a grill pan over medium heat, add the sandwiches. Cook for 3-4 minutes on each side or until the biscuits are golden brown. Remove the skillet from the heat and serve.

Anytime Bacon, Egg & Cheese Sandwiches

Makes 4 servings

1/2 cup sour cream
8 bread slices
4 green onions, chopped
4 slices American cheese, 1 oz. size
2 hard boiled eggs, peeled & cut into 1/2" slices
8 bacon slices, cooked
1/4 cup softened unsalted butter

Spread the sour cream on one side of 4 bread slices. Place the green onions over the sour cream. Place the American cheese, hard boiled eggs and bacon over the sour cream. Place the remaining bread slices on the sandwiches. Spread the butter on the outside of the sandwiches.

In a skillet over medium heat, add the sandwiches. Cook for 3 minutes on each side or until golden brown. Remove the skillet from the heat and serve. You can cook the sandwiches on a panini press instead of using a skillet.

Prosciutto, Cheddar & Egg Breakfast Biscuits

Makes 6 servings

2 1/2 cups Bisquick
1/2 cup plus 2 tbs. whole milk
3 tbs. melted unsalted butter
1 tbs. minced fresh chives
6 eggs
1/8 tsp. salt
2 oz. thinly sliced prosciutto, cut into thin strips
2 green onions, chopped
1 tbs. unsalted butter
1/2 cup shredded cheddar cheese

Preheat the oven to 425°. In a mixing bowl, add the Bisquick, 1/2 cup milk, butter and chives. Stir just until the dough is moistened and forms into a ball. Lightly flour your work surface. Place the dough on the surface. Knead 8 times or until the dough holds together.

Pat the dough to 3/4" thickness. Using a 2 1/2" biscuit cutter, cut out the biscuits. Cut the biscuits as close together as possible. Place the biscuits, 2" apart, on a baking sheet. Roll the dough scraps to cut out all the biscuits.

Bake for 12-15 minutes or until the biscuits are golden brown. Remove from the oven. While the biscuits are baking, make the eggs. In a mixing bowl, add the eggs, 2 tablespoons milk and salt. Whisk until combined and set aside for the moment.

In a skillet over medium heat, add the prosciutto and green onions. Stir constantly and cook until the prosciutto begins to brown. Add the butter to the skillet. When the butter melts, add the eggs. Stir until the eggs are set. Add the cheddar cheese to the skillet. Stir until combined and remove from the heat.

Place the biscuits on a serving platter. Split the biscuits open and spoon the eggs on the bottom biscuits. Place the top biscuits over the eggs and serve.

Italian Sausage & Egg Croissants

Makes 8 servings

1 cup crumbled blue cheese
1 jalapeno pepper, seeded & minced
1 tsp. dried basil
1 tsp. dried oregano
1 tsp. dried parsley flakes
1 lb. ground Italian sausage
8 eggs
3 tbs. whole milk
1/8 tsp. salt
1/8 tsp. black pepper
3 tbs. unsalted butter
1/2 cup mayonnaise
8 croissants, split
1 large tomato, cut into 8 slices
1 avocado, peeled & cut into 8 slices

In a mixing bowl, add the blue cheese, jalapeno pepper, basil, oregano and parsley flakes. Toss until combined. Add the Italian sausage to the bowl. Using your hands, mix until combined. Form into 8 patties.

In a large skillet over medium heat, add the patties. Cook for 4-5 minutes on each side or until the patties are no longer pink and browned. Remove the skillet from the heat and drain the sausage patties on paper towels. Keep the patties warm while you cook the eggs.

In a mixing bowl, add the eggs, milk, salt and black pepper. Whisk until combined. Add the butter to a skillet over medium heat. When the butter melts, add the eggs. When the eggs are set on the bottom and sides of the skillet, lift the edges with a spatula to let the uncooked eggs run underneath. Cook for 4 minutes or until the eggs are set on the top. Remove the skillet from the heat. Cut the eggs into 8 wedges.

Place the bottom croissants on a serving platter. Spread the mayonnaise over the bottom croissants. Place a sausage patty over the mayonnaise on each croissant. Place an egg wedge over the sausage on each croissant. Place one tomato slice and one avocado slice over the eggs on each croissant. Place the top croissants over the sandwiches and serve.

Omelet Croissants

Makes 2 servings

3 eggs
1 tbs. water
1 tsp. instant chicken bouillon granules
1 finely chopped green onion
2 tbs. finely chopped red bell pepper
1/4 tsp. lemon pepper seasoning
1/2 tsp. unsalted butter
4 teaspoons prepared ranch salad dressing
2 croissants, split
4 slices cooked Canadian bacon
4 slices Muenster cheese
1/2 cup fresh arugula
4 thin slices tomato

In a small bowl, add the eggs, water and chicken bouillon. Whisk until combined. In a small skillet over medium heat, add the green onion, red bell pepper, lemon pepper and butter. Saute for 4 minutes.

Add the eggs to the skillet. As the eggs set around the edges, gently lift the edges to allow the uncooked eggs to run underneath. Cook about 3-4 minutes or until the eggs are completely set. Remove the skillet from the heat.

Cut the omelet in half. Spread the ranch dressing on the cut sides of the croissants. Place an omelet half over the bottom of each croissants. Place the Canadian bacon slices over the omelet. Place the Muenster cheese over the Canadian bacon. Place the arugula over the cheese. Place the tomato slices over the top. Place the tops on the croissants.

Spray a skillet with non stick cooking spray and place over medium heat. When the skillet is hot, add the sandwiches. Cook for 2-3 minutes on each side or until the croissants are toasted and the cheese melted. Remove the skillet from the heat and serve.

Spicy Scrambled Egg Sandwiches

Makes 4 servings

1/3 cup chopped green bell pepper
1/4 cup chopped onion
3 eggs
4 egg whites
1 tbs. water
1/4 tsp. salt
1/4 tsp. ground mustard
1/8 tsp. black pepper
1/8 tsp. Tabasco sauce
1/3 cup cooked whole kernel corn
1/4 cup crumbled cooked bacon
4 English muffins, split & toasted

Spray a 10" skillet with non stick cooking spray. Place the skillet over medium heat. Add the green bell pepper and onion to the skillet. Saute for 6 minutes or until the vegetables are tender. In a mixing bowl, add the eggs, egg whites, water, salt, ground mustard, black pepper and Tabasco sauce. Whisk until combined and add to the skillet. Sprinkle the corn and bacon over the eggs. Stir frequently and cook for 5 minutes or until the eggs are set and scrambled. Remove the skillet from the heat.

Place the bottom English muffins on a serving platter. Spoon the eggs over the muffin bottoms. Place the top muffins on the sandwiches and serve.

Ham Breakfast Wraps

Makes 4 servings

6 eggs
2 tbs. whole milk
1/4 tsp. black pepper
1 tbs. vegetable oil
1 cup shredded cheddar cheese
3/4 cup diced cooked ham
4 warm flour tortillas, 8" size

In a small bowl, add the eggs, milk and black pepper. Whisk until combined. In a skillet over medium heat, add the vegetable oil. When the oil is hot, add the eggs. Stir frequently and cook about 4 minutes or until the eggs are set and scrambled. Add the cheddar cheese and ham to the skillet. Stir until combined. Remove the skillet from the heat. Spoon the egg filling down the center of each tortilla. Roll the tortillas ups and serve.

Fried Egg & Pancetta Sandwiches

Makes 4 servings

4 slices challah bread, 1/2" thick
2 tbs. melted unsalted butter
1 oz. pkg. hollandaise sauce, prepared
1/4 tsp. grated lemon zest
1 1/2 tsp. fresh lemon juice
2 cups arugula
1/2 cup fresh parsley leaves
1/4 cup thinly sliced red onion
3 tsp. olive oil
4 eggs
1/4 tsp. salt
1/4 tsp. black pepper
12 pancetta slices, cooked
2 tbs. chopped sun dried tomatoes

Preheat the oven to the broiler position. Brush both sides of the bread with the melted butter. Place the bread on a broiler pan. Broil for 1-2 minutes on each side or until golden brown. Remove from the oven.

After the hollandaise sauce is prepared, stir in the lemon zest and 1/2 teaspoon lemon juice. Keep the sauce warm while you prepare the eggs. In a small bowl, add the arugula, parsley, onion, 2 teaspoons olive oil and 1 teaspoon lemon juice. Toss until combined.

Add 1 teaspoon olive oil to a skillet over medium heat. When the oil is hot, break the eggs into the skillet. Sprinkle the salt and black pepper over the eggs. Cook for 2 minutes on each side or until the eggs are done to your taste. Remove the skillet from the heat.

Spread the arugula over one side of each bread slice. Place the pancetta over the arugula. Place one egg on each sandwich. Spoon the hollandaise sauce over the top. Sprinkle the sun dried tomatoes over the sauce and serve.

Scrambled Egg Muffin Sliders

Makes 12 servings

2 cups self rising white cornmeal mix
1 tbs. granulated sugar
1 1/2 cups buttermilk
9 eggs
4 tbs. melted unsalted butter
1 cup shredded sharp cheddar cheese
6 bacon slices, cooked & crumbled
1/2 tsp. Creole seasoning
1 tbs. unsalted butter

Preheat the oven to 425°. Spray a 12 cup muffin tin with non stick cooking spray. Place the muffin tin in the oven until hot. While the muffin tin is heating, make the batter.

In a mixing bowl, add the cornmeal mix and granulated sugar. Stir until combined. Add the buttermilk and 1 egg to the bowl. Stir only until the batter is moistened. Add 4 tablespoons butter, cheddar cheese and bacon to the bowl. Stir until the batter is moistened and combined.

Spoon the batter into the muffin cups filling them almost full. Bake for 15-20 minutes or until the muffins are golden brown. Remove from the oven and cool for 10 minutes in the muffin tin. Remove from the muffin tin.

In a mixing bowl, add 8 eggs and the Creole seasoning. Whisk until combined. In a skillet over medium heat, add 1 tablespoon butter. When the butter melts, add the eggs. Stir frequently and cook until the eggs are set. Remove from the heat.

Split the muffins in half. Place the bottom halves on a serving platter. Spoon the eggs over the bottom muffins. Place the top muffins over the eggs and serve.

Mexican Breakfast Burritos

Makes 4 servings

6 eggs
1/8 tsp. black pepper
1/3 cup rinsed & drained black beans
2 tbs. sliced green onion
2 flour tortillas, 10" size
3 tbs. shredded cheddar cheese
3 tbs. salsa

Spray a skillet with non stick cooking spray. In a small bowl, add the eggs and black pepper. Whisk until combined. Place the skillet over medium heat. When the skillet is hot, add the eggs. Stir frequently and cook about 4 minutes or until the eggs are set.

Add the black beans and green onions to the skillet. Stir until combined and cook about 1 minute or until the beans are hot. Remove the skillet from the heat. Spoon the eggs down the center of each tortilla. Sprinkle the cheddar cheese over the egg filling. Roll the tortillas up and place on a serving platter. Cut each tortilla in half. Spoon the salsa over the top and serve.

Green Chili Breakfast Burritos

Makes 6 servings

6 eggs
3 egg whites
1 jalapeno pepper, seeded & minced
1/8 tsp. cayenne pepper
8 oz. ground turkey breakfast sausage
3/4 cup shredded Mexican cheese blend
4 oz. can chopped green chiles, drained
6 warm whole wheat flour tortillas, 8" size
6 tbs. salsa

In a small bowl, add the eggs, egg whites, jalapeno pepper and cayenne pepper. Whisk until combined. In a large skillet over medium heat, add the sausage. Stir frequently to break the sausage into crumbles as it cooks. Cook for 8 minutes or until the sausage is well browned and no longer pink. Drain off any excess grease.

Push the sausage to the edges of the skillet. Pour the eggs in the center of the skillet. Stir constantly and cook until the eggs are set and scrambled. Add the Mexican cheese blend and green chiles to the skillet. Stir until combined and the cheese melts. Remove from the heat. Spoon 1/3 cup filling down the center of each tortilla. Fold the tortillas up to form a burrito and place on a serving platter. Spoon 1 tablespoon salsa over each burrito and serve.

Sausage, Egg & Cheese Burritos

Makes 6 burritos

8 oz. ground pork sausage
5 eggs
1 tbs. milk
Salt and black pepper to taste
3/4 cup shredded sharp cheddar cheese
6 warm flour tortillas, 6" size
Salsa or Tabasco sauce, optional

In a skillet over medium heat, add the sausage. Stir frequently to break the sausage into crumbles as it cooks. Cook for 6 minutes or until the sausage is well browned and no longer pink. Remove the skillet from the heat and drain the sausage on paper towels.

Drain off all but 1 tablespoon sausage drippings from the skillet. In a mixing bowl, add the eggs, milk and salt and black pepper to taste. Whisk until combined. Place the skillet back on the stove over medium heat. When the skillet is hot, add the eggs. Stir frequently and cook until the eggs are set and scrambled. Remove the skillet from the heat and stir the sausage into the eggs.

Spoon the egg filling down the center of the tortillas. Sprinkle the cheddar cheese over the filling. Roll the tortillas up and serve with salsa or Tabasco sauce as desired.

Sausage Monterey Jack Breakfast Burritos

Makes 12 servings

1/2 cup unsalted butter
3/4 cup chopped onion
1/2 cup chopped green bell pepper
1 lb. ground pork sausage
12 beaten eggs
Salt & black pepper to taste
12 warm flour tortillas, 8" size
1 cup shredded Monterey Jack cheese
1 cup picante sauce

In a skillet over medium heat, add 1/4 cup butter. When the butter melts, add the onion and green bell pepper. Saute for 5 minutes. Remove the skillet from the heat.

In a skillet over medium heat, add the sausage. Stir frequently and cook about 8 minutes or until the sausage is well browned and no longer pink. Remove the skillet from the heat and add the sausage to the onion and green bell pepper. Wipe the skillet clean with a paper towel.

Add 1/4 cup butter to the skillet and place over medium heat. When the butter melts, add the eggs. Season to taste with salt and black pepper. Stir frequently and cook about 6 minutes or until the eggs are set and scrambled. Remove the skillet from the heat. Add the sausage, onions and green bell peppers to the eggs. Stir until combined.

Spoon 1/2 cup egg filling down the center of each tortilla. Sprinkle the Monterey Jack cheese over the filling. Roll the tortillas up and serve with the picante sauce.

Egg Baguette Bake

Makes 5 servings

1 lb. Italian baguette, 12" x 4" size
4 oz. sweet ground Italian sausage
1/2 cup chopped red bell pepper
1/4 cup sliced green onions
5 beaten eggs
1/3 cup half and half cream
1/2 cup minced fresh basil
3/4 cup shredded mozzarella cheese

Preheat the oven to 350°. Line a 9 x 13 baking pan with parchment paper. Cut a thin wedge from the top of the baguette. Remove the bread from the inside of the loaf leaving about a 1/2" bread on the sides of the loaf. Use the removed bread for another use. Place the baguette on the baking pan.

In a skillet over medium heat, add the sausage, red bell pepper and green onions. Stir frequently to break the sausage into crumbles as it cooks. Cook for 6 minutes or until the sausage is well browned and no longer pink. Remove the skillet from the heat and drain off the excess grease.

Add the sausage to a mixing bowl. Add the eggs, half and half cream, basil and 1/2 cup mozzarella cheese to the bowl. Whisk until combined and pour into the bread shell. Sprinkle 1/4 cup mozzarella cheese over the top.

Bake for 35 minutes or until the eggs are set in the center of the loaf. Remove from the oven and cool for 5 minutes before slicing.

Tortilla Wrapped Asparagus Omelet

Makes 1 serving

1 egg
2 egg whites
1 tbs. whole milk
2 tsp. grated Parmesan cheese
1/8 tsp. black pepper
4 fresh asparagus spears, trimmed & chopped
1 tsp. unsalted butter
1 green onion, chopped
8" flour tortilla, warmed

In a small bowl, add the egg, egg whites, milk, Parmesan cheese and black pepper. Whisk until combined. Spray a small skillet with non stick cooking spray and place over medium heat. Add the asparagus to the skillet. Saute for 4 minutes or until the asparagus spears are tender. Remove the asparagus from the skillet and set aside.

Add the butter to the skillet. When the butter melts, add the eggs. Cook until the eggs are set on the bottom and sides. Gently lift the set edges of the eggs to allow the uncooked egg to run underneath. Cook for 2-3 minutes or until the eggs are completely set.

Sprinkle the asparagus and green onion over one half of the omelet. Fold the other half over the vegetables. Remove the skillet from the heat. Slide the omelet on one side of the tortilla. Fold the tortilla over the omelet and serve.

Spanish Brunch Wraps

Makes 2 servings

3 eggs
1 tbs. shredded Manchego cheese
1/2 tsp. dried oregano
1/4 tsp. black pepper
1 tbs. chopped green onions
1 tbs. chopped jarred roasted red bell peppers
3 tsp. olive oil
2 warm sun dried tomato tortillas, 8" size
1/4 cup tapenade
1 1/2 tsp. minced fresh parsley
1 1/2 tsp. lemon juice
1 garlic clove, minced
1/2 tsp. drained capers

In a small bowl, add the eggs, Manchego cheese, oregano and black pepper. Whisk until combined. In a small skillet over medium heat, add the green onions, red bell peppers and 1 1/2 teaspoons olive oil. Saute for 3 minutes. Add the eggs to the skillet. Stir frequently and cook until the eggs are scrambled and set. Remove the skillet from the heat.

Spread the tapenade on one side of each tortilla. Spoon the egg filling in the center of the tortillas. Roll the wraps up and place on a serving platter. In a small bowl, add the parsley, lemon juice, garlic and capers. Stir until combined and spoon over the wraps.

Italian Sausage & Egg Breakfast Burrito

Makes 6 servings

12 oz. ground Italian sausage
1/2 cup finely chopped green bell pepper
1/2 cup finely chopped onion
1 tomato, chopped
4 eggs
6 egg whites
1 cup chopped fresh spinach
6 flour tortillas, 8" size
1 cup shredded cheddar cheese

In a skillet over medium heat, add the Italian sausage, green bell pepper, onion and tomato. Stir frequently to break the sausage into crumbles as it cooks. Cook for 6-8 minutes or until the sausage is well browned and no longer pink. Remove the sausage from the skillet using a slotted spoon and drain on paper towels. Drain off any excess grease.

In a mixing bowl, add the eggs, egg whites and spinach. Whisk until combined and add to the skillet. Stir frequently and cook about 4 minutes or until the eggs are set. Remove the skillet from the heat and add the sausage to the skillet. Stir until combined.

Spoon about 3/4 cup egg filling down the center of each tortilla. Sprinkle 2 tablespoons cheddar cheese over the filling in each tortilla. Roll the tortillas up and serve.

Breakfast Egg & Sausage Quesadillas

Makes 6 servings

12 oz. ground pork sausage
1 tbs. unsalted butter
10 beaten eggs
1 1/2 cups shredded Pepper Jack cheese
1/4 tsp. salt
1/8 tsp. black pepper
6 warm flour tortillas, 8" size

In a skillet over medium heat, add the sausage. Stir frequently to break the sausage into crumbles as it cooks. Cook for 8 minutes or until the sausage is well browned and no longer pink. Remove the skillet from the heat. Drain the sausage on paper towels. Wipe the skillet clean.

Add the butter to the skillet and place over medium heat. When the butter melts, add the eggs. Stir frequently and cook for 5 minutes or until the eggs are almost set. Add the sausage, Pepper Jack cheese, salt and black pepper to the skillet. Stir until combined and cook until the eggs are set and scrambled. Remove the skillet from the heat.

Spoon the eggs down the center of each tortilla. Roll the tortillas up and serve.

Huevos Rancheros Quesadillas

Makes 4 servings

4 beaten eggs
1/4 tsp. salt
1/4 tsp. black pepper
1 tbs. unsalted butter
15 oz. can black beans, rinsed & drained
1 tomato, sliced
1/3 cup sliced black olives
2 tbs. chopped red onion
1 cup salsa
4 flour tortillas, 8" size
1 cup shredded cheddar cheese

In a small bowl, add the eggs, salt and black pepper. In a skillet over medium heat, add the butter. When the butter melts, add the eggs. Stir frequently and cook about 4 minutes or until the eggs are set and scrambled. Remove the skillet from the heat.

In a skillet over low heat, add the black beans, tomato, olives and onion. Saute for 4 minutes. Add the salsa to the skillet. Stir frequently and cook for 5-7 minutes or until the sauce thickens. Remove the skillet from the heat.

Spoon the eggs on one half of each tortilla. Spoon the black beans over the eggs. Sprinkle the cheddar cheese over the top. Fold the other half of the tortilla over the filling.

In a large skillet over medium heat, add the quesadillas. Cook for 2-3 minutes on each side or until golden brown. Remove from the heat and serve.

Scotch Eggs

Makes 6 servings

1 lb. ground pork sausage
6 hard boiled eggs, peeled
1 beaten egg
3/4 cup crushed cornflakes

Divide the sausage into 6 equal portions. Wrap each portion around a hard boiled egg. Preheat the oven to 400°. Add the beaten egg to a small bowl. Add the cornflakes to a small bowl. Dip each piece in the egg allowing the excess liquid to drip off back into the bowl. Roll each piece in the cornflakes.

Spray a baking sheet with non stick cooking spray. Place the eggs on the baking sheet. Bake for 30-35 minutes or until the sausage is browned and no longer pink. Turn every 10 minutes to ensure even cooking. Remove from the oven. Remove the eggs from the pan and drain on paper towels. Serve hot.

Farmer Egg Salad

This is great for brunch, lunch or dinner.

Makes 8 servings

8 thick bacon slices, cooked & crumbled
8 cups baby arugula
4 cups chopped romaine lettuce
2 cups thinly sliced radicchio
2 cups challah bread cubes, toasted
1/2 cup shaved Parmesan cheese
8 hard boiled eggs, peeled & halved
1 1/4 cups freshly grated Parmesan cheese
1/2 cup red wine vinegar
4 anchovy fillets
1 tsp. grated lemon zest
1 tbs. fresh lemon juice
1 garlic clove, minced
1 tsp. Dijon mustard
1 tsp. Worcestershire sauce
1/2 cup olive oil
Salt and black pepper to taste

In a mixing bowl, add the bacon, arugula, romaine lettuce, radicchio, challah bread cubes and shaved Parmesan cheese. Toss until combined. Spoon into serving plates. Place 2 egg halves over each salad.

In a food processor, add 1 1/4 cups freshly grated Parmesan cheese, red wine vinegar, anchovy fillets, lemon zest, lemon juice, garlic, Dijon mustard and Worcestershire sauce. Process until smooth. With the food processor running, slowly add the olive oil. Process until combined. Season to taste with salt and black pepper. Drizzle the dressing to taste over the salads and serve.

Egg Salad Sandwich Filling

Makes 3 cups

8 hard boiled eggs, peeled & finely chopped
2/3 cup mayonnaise
1/2 cup finely chopped celery
1/4 cup minced fresh chives
2 tbs. minced red onion
1 tbs. chopped fresh tarragon
1 tsp. black pepper
1/2 tsp. season salt

Add all the ingredients to a mixing bowl. Stir until combined. Refrigerate for 1 hour before serving. Store the egg salad covered in the refrigerator.

Ham & Egg Salad Sandwich Filling

Makes 6 sandwiches

6 hard boiled eggs, peeled & chopped
1 cup cooked diced ham
1/2 cup finely chopped celery
1 tbs. minced onion
1/2 cup mayonnaise
2 tsp. prepared mustard
1/2 tsp. salt
1/4 tsp. black pepper

Add all the ingredients to a serving bowl. Stir until combined. Cover the bowl and refrigerate at least 1 hour before serving.

Shrimp Egg Salad

Makes 1 1/2 cups

4 oz. cooked shrimp, finely chopped
2 hard boiled eggs, chopped
1/4 cup chopped celery
3 tbs. mayonnaise
1 tsp. lemon juice
1/4 tsp. onion powder
1/4 tsp. salt
1/8 tsp. lemon pepper seasoning

Add all the ingredients to a serving bowl. Stir until combined. Cover the bowl and refrigerate for 1 hour before serving. Serve with crackers or use as a sandwich spread.

Crab Egg Cracker Spread

Makes 2 1/2 cups

1/3 cup mayonnaise
1/3 cup chili sauce
1 tbs. prepared horseradish
1 garlic clove, minced
1/2 tsp. prepared mustard
1/2 tsp. Tabasco sauce
1/2 tsp. salt
1 1/2 cups flaked cooked crabmeat
2 hard boiled eggs, chopped

In a serving bowl, add the mayonnaise, chili sauce, horseradish, garlic, mustard, Tabasco sauce and salt. Stir until combined. Stir in the crab and eggs. Cover the bowl and refrigerate for 1 hour before serving. Serve with your favorite crackers.

5 DEVILED EGGS

Who does not love deviled eggs? They are a southern specialty. We eat them at barbecues, potlucks, breakfast and just about any occasion or meal. Included are many different variations on deviled eggs.

Cajun Spiced Deviled Eggs

Makes 10 eggs

5 hard boiled eggs, peeled
1 1/2 tbs. Dijon mustard
1 1/2 tbs. mayonnaise
5 pimento stuffed green olives, halved
1 tsp. Cajun seasoning

Cut the eggs in half lengthwise and remove the yolks. Place the yolks in a small bowl. Mash the egg yolks with a fork. Add the Dijon mustard and mayonnaise to the egg yolks. Stir until well combined.

Spoon or pipe the egg yolks into the center of the egg whites. Place the eggs on a serving platter. Place a green olive half on each egg. Sprinkle the Cajun seasoning over the eggs and serve.

Smoked Salmon & Cream Cheese Deviled Eggs

Makes 12 servings

6 eggs
3 tbs. minced smoked salmon
3 tbs. minced green onions
3 tbs. softened cream cheese
1 tbs. sour cream
1 tsp. Dijon mustard
2 tsp. lemon juice
3/4 tsp. salt
1/8 tsp. black pepper

Add the eggs to a sauce pan over medium heat. Cover the eggs with water and bring the eggs to a full boil. Place a lid on the pan and remove the pan from the heat. Let the eggs sit for 15 minutes. Drain the water from the eggs. Add cold water to cover the eggs in the pan. Let the eggs sit until cool.

Peel the eggs. Cut each egg in half lengthwise and remove the yolks. Place the yolks into a bowl. Set the egg whites aside for now. Add the salmon, green onions, cream cheese, sour cream, Dijon mustard, lemon juice, salt and black pepper to the bowl. Mash the yolks and stir until combined.

Spoon the filling into the egg whites. Place the eggs on a serving platter. Cover the platter and refrigerate for 2 hours before serving. Store the eggs in the refrigerator no longer than 2 days.

Pecan Stuffed Deviled Eggs

Makes 6 servings

6 hard boiled eggs, peeled
1/4 cup mayonnaise
1 tsp. grated onion
1 tsp. white vinegar
1/2 tsp. chopped fresh parsley
1/2 tsp. dry mustard
1/8 tsp. salt
1/3 cup chopped pecans

Cut the eggs in half lengthwise and remove the yolks. Place the yolks in a small bowl. Mash the egg yolks with a fork. Add the mayonnaise, onion, white vinegar, parsley, dry mustard, salt and pecans to the egg yolks. Stir until well combined.

Spoon or pipe the egg yolks into the center of the egg whites. Place the eggs on a serving platter. Serve the eggs chilled or freshly made. Store leftovers covered in the refrigerator up to 2 days.

Spicy Sweet Deviled Eggs

Makes 24 eggs

12 hard boiled eggs, peeled
1/2 cup mayonnaise
3 tbs. mango chutney
1/2 tsp. cayenne pepper
Minced fresh chives, optional

Cut the eggs in half lengthwise and remove the yolks. Place the yolks in a small bowl. Mash the egg yolks with a fork. Add the mayonnaise, mango chutney and cayenne pepper to the egg yolks. Stir until well combined.

Spoon or pipe the egg yolks into the center of the egg whites. Place the eggs on a serving platter. Sprinkle the chives over the top if desired. Serve the eggs chilled or freshly made. Store leftovers covered in the refrigerator up to 2 days.

Tex Mex Deviled Eggs

Makes 1 dozen

6 hard boiled eggs, peeled
1 tbs. diced green onion
1 tbs. chopped fresh cilantro
1 jalapeño pepper, seeded and finely chopped
1/4 cup mayonnaise
1 tsp. yellow prepared mustard
1/2 tsp. salt
1/4 cup shredded cheddar cheese
Chili powder, optional

Cut the eggs in half lengthwise and remove the yolks. Place the yolks in a small bowl. Mash the egg yolks with a fork. Add the green onion, cilantro, jalapeño pepper, mayonnaise, mustard, salt and cheddar cheese to the egg yolks. Stir until well combined.

Spoon or pipe the egg yolks into the center of the egg whites. Place the eggs on a serving platter. Sprinkle the chili powder over the top if desired. Cover the eggs and chill for 3 hours before serving. Store leftovers covered in the refrigerator up to 2 days.

Bacon Stuffed Eggs

Makes 12 servings

12 hard boiled eggs, peeled
3 oz. pkg. cream cheese, softened
2 tsp. Worcestershire sauce
1/4 tsp. salt
1/2 tsp. black pepper
4 bacon slices, cooked and crumbled

Cut the eggs in half lengthwise and remove the yolks. Place the yolks in a small bowl. Mash the egg yolks with a fork. Add the cream cheese, Worcestershire sauce, salt, black pepper and bacon to the egg yolks. Stir until well combined.

Spoon or pipe the egg yolks into the center of the egg whites. Place the eggs on a serving platter. Serve the eggs chilled or freshly made. Store leftovers covered in the refrigerator up to 2 days.

Blue Cheese Deviled Eggs

Makes 12 servings

12 hard boiled eggs, peeled
1/2 cup crumbled blue cheese
1/2 cup sour cream
1 tbs. white vinegar
1/4 tsp. salt, optional

Taste the filling for the eggs before adding the salt. Some blue cheese is saltier than others, so adjust the salt to taste. Cut the eggs in half lengthwise and remove the yolks. Place the yolks in a large bowl. Mash the egg yolks with a fork. Add the blue cheese, sour cream, white vinegar and salt to the egg yolks. Stir until well combined.

Spoon or pipe the egg yolks into the center of the egg whites. Place the eggs on a serving platter. Chill the eggs for 4 hours before serving. Store leftovers covered in the refrigerator up to 2 days.

Cream Cheese Yogurt Deviled Eggs

Makes 2 dozen

12 eggs
1/3 cup plain Greek yogurt
2 oz. cream cheese, softened
1 tbs. chopped fresh parsley
1 tsp. Dijon mustard
1/8 tsp. salt

Add the eggs to a large sauce pan over medium heat. Cover the eggs with water and bring the eggs to a full boil. Boil for 1 minute. Remove the pan from the heat and place a lid on the pan. Let the eggs sit for 10 minutes. Drain all the water from the pan.

Run cold water over the eggs until cool. Peel the eggs and slice in half lengthwise. Carefully remove the yolks and place in a small bowl. Mash the yolks with a fork. Add the yogurt, cream cheese, parsley, Dijon mustard and salt to the yolks. Stir until well combined. Spoon the filling into the egg white halves. Serve freshly made or refrigerate until chilled. Store the eggs in the refrigerator up to 2 days.

Green Pea Deviled Eggs

Makes 2 dozen

12 eggs
1/2 cup blanched fresh green peas, chopped
4 bacon slices, cooked & crumbled
1/4 cup mayonnaise
2 tbs. minced red onion
2 tbs. sour cream
1 tbs. chopped fresh mint
1/4 tsp. salt
1/8 tsp. black pepper

Add the eggs to a large sauce pan over medium heat. Cover the eggs with water and bring the eggs to a full boil. Boil for 1 minute. Remove the pan from the heat and place a lid on the pan. Let the eggs sit for 10 minutes. Drain all the water from the pan.

Run cold water over the eggs until cool. Peel the eggs and slice in half lengthwise. Carefully remove the yolks and place in a small bowl. Mash the yolks with a fork. Add the green peas to the yolks. Slightly mash the green peas. Add the bacon, mayonnaise, red onion, sour cream, mint, salt and black pepper to the yolks. Stir until well combined. Spoon the filling into the egg white halves. Serve freshly made or refrigerate until chilled. Store the eggs in the refrigerator up to 2 days.

Mexican Deviled Eggs

Makes 6 servings

6 hard boiled eggs, peeled
1/4 cup mayonnaise
2 tbs. pickled jalapeño slices, minced
1 tbs. yellow prepared mustard
1/8 tsp. salt
1/4 tsp. ground cumin

Cut the eggs in half lengthwise and remove the yolks. Place the yolks in a small bowl. Mash the egg yolks with a fork. Add the mayonnaise, jalapeño, mustard, salt and cumin to the egg yolks. Stir until well combined.

Spoon or pipe the egg yolks into the center of the egg whites. Place the eggs on a serving platter. Serve the eggs chilled or freshly made. Store leftovers covered in the refrigerator up to 2 days.

Shrimp and Bacon Deviled Eggs

Makes 12 servings

12 hard boiled eggs, peeled
3/4 cup mayonnaise
1 tbs. Dijon mustard
1/2 tsp. cayenne pepper
1/4 tsp. salt
1 cup chopped cooked shrimp
1/3 cup crumbled cooked bacon
1/4 cup chopped fresh chives

Cut the eggs in half lengthwise and remove the yolks. Place the yolks in a bowl. Mash the egg yolks with a fork. Add the mayonnaise, Dijon mustard, cayenne pepper, salt, shrimp, bacon and chives to the egg yolks. Stir until well combined.

Spoon or pipe the egg yolks into the center of the egg whites. Place the eggs on a serving platter. Chill the eggs for 4 hours before serving. Store leftovers covered in the refrigerator up to 2 days.

Shrimp Remoulade Deviled Eggs

Makes 2 dozen

3/4 cup mayonnaise
3 tbs. minced green onions
1 tbs. minced fresh parsley
1 1/2 tbs. Creole mustard
2 tsp. lemon zest
2 garlic cloves, minced
1/4 tsp. salt
1/4 tsp. cayenne pepper
12 eggs
1 cup finely chopped cooked shrimp

In a small bowl, add the mayonnaise, green onions, parsley, Creole mustard, lemon zest, garlic, salt and cayenne pepper. Stir until combined. Cover the bowl and refrigerate for 2 hours. Add the eggs to a large sauce pan over medium heat. Cover the eggs with water and bring the eggs to a full boil. Boil for 1 minute. Remove the pan from the heat and place a lid on the pan. Let the eggs sit for 10 minutes. Drain all the water from the pan.

Run cold water over the eggs until cool. Peel the eggs and slice in half lengthwise. Carefully remove the yolks and place in a small bowl. Mash the yolks with a fork. Add the yolks and shrimp to the mayonnaise mixture. Stir until well combined. Spoon the filling into the egg white halves. Serve freshly made or refrigerate until chilled. Store the eggs in the refrigerator up to 2 days.

Smoky Pimento Cheese Deviled Eggs

Makes 2 dozen

12 eggs
1/4 cup mayonnaise
3/4 cup shredded smoked cheddar cheese
1/4 cup chopped jarred roasted red bell peppers, drained
1 tbs. Dijon mustard
Pinch of cayenne pepper

Add the eggs to a large sauce pan over medium heat. Cover the eggs with water and bring the eggs to a full boil. Boil for 1 minute. Remove the pan from the heat and place a lid on the pan. Let the eggs sit for 10 minutes. Drain all the water from the pan.

Run cold water over the eggs until cool. Peel the eggs and slice in half lengthwise. Carefully remove the yolks and place in a small bowl. Mash the yolks with a fork. Add the mayonnaise, cheddar cheese, red bell peppers, Dijon mustard and cayenne pepper to the yolks. Stir until well combined. Spoon the filling into the egg white halves. Serve freshly made or refrigerate until chilled. Store the eggs in the refrigerator up to 2 days.

Spicy Deviled Eggs

Makes 2 dozen

12 hard boiled eggs, peeled
1/2 cup mayonnaise
1 tbs. chopped fresh parsley
2 tbs. sour cream
1 tsp. spicy brown mustard
1/8 tsp. salt
1 tbs. minced green onion
1 tsp. Sriracha chili sauce

Slice the eggs in half lengthwise. Carefully remove the yolks and place in a small bowl. Mash the yolks with a fork. Add the mayonnaise, parsley, sour cream, mustard, salt, green onion and Sriracha sauce to the yolks. Stir until well combined. Spoon the filling into the egg white halves. Serve freshly made or refrigerate until chilled. Store the eggs in the refrigerator up to 2 days.

Cilantro Tuna Salad Deviled Eggs

Makes 12 servings

12 eggs
1/2 cup mayonnaise
4 cans drained tuna in water, 5 oz. size
1 cup chopped onion
1 celery rib, chopped
1/2 cup minced fresh cilantro
1/2 cup dill pickle relish
1/4 tsp. lemon juice
1/2 tsp. celery seeds
1/4 tsp. black pepper

You will not use all the tuna filling for this recipe. Refrigerate the remaining tuna filling and serve on sandwiches or with crackers for another meal. Add the eggs to a large sauce pan over medium heat. Cover the eggs with water and bring the eggs to a full boil. Boil for 1 minute. Remove the pan from the heat and place a lid on the pan. Let the eggs sit for 10 minutes. Drain all the water from the pan.

Run cold water over the eggs until cool. Peel the eggs and slice in half lengthwise. Carefully remove the yolks and place in a mixing bowl. Mash the yolks with a fork. Flake the tuna with a fork. Add the tuna, onion, celery, cilantro, dill pickle relish, lemon juice, celery seeds and black pepper to the yolks. Stir until well combined. Spoon the filling into the egg white halves. Serve freshly made or refrigerate until chilled. Store the eggs in the refrigerator up to 2 days.

Deluxe Deviled Eggs

Makes 2 dozen

12 hard boiled eggs
2 oz. cream cheese, softened
1/4 cup mayonnaise
1 tbs. spicy brown mustard
1/2 tsp. cider vinegar
1/8 tsp. salt
1/8 tsp. onion powder

Peel the eggs and slice in half lengthwise. Carefully remove the yolks and place in a mixing bowl. Mash the yolks with a fork. Add the cream cheese, mayonnaise, mustard, cider vinegar, salt and onion powder to the yolks. Stir until well combined. Spoon the filling into the egg white halves. Serve freshly made or refrigerate until chilled. Store the eggs in the refrigerator up to 2 days.

Creole Shrimp Deviled Eggs

Makes 2 dozen

12 eggs
1/3 cup plain Greek yogurt
2 oz. cream cheese, softened
1 tbs. chopped fresh parsley
1 tsp. Dijon mustard
1/8 tsp. salt
1/2 cup finely chopped cooked shrimp
3 tbs. sauteed chopped green bell pepper
1 minced green onion
1/4 tsp. Creole seasoning
1/4 tsp. Tabasco sauce

Add the eggs to a large sauce pan over medium heat. Cover the eggs with water and bring the eggs to a full boil. Boil for 1 minute. Remove the pan from the heat and place a lid on the pan. Let the eggs sit for 10 minutes. Drain all the water from the pan.

Run cold water over the eggs until cool. Peel the eggs and slice in half lengthwise. Carefully remove the yolks and place in a small bowl. Mash the yolks with a fork. Add the yogurt, cream cheese, parsley, Dijon mustard, salt, shrimp, green bell pepper, green onion, Creole seasoning and Tabasco sauce to the yolks. Stir until well combined. Spoon the filling into the egg white halves. Serve freshly made or refrigerate until chilled. Store the eggs in the refrigerator up to 2 days.

Curry Deviled Eggs

Makes 12 servings

6 hard boiled eggs, peeled
3 tbs. mayonnaise
1 tsp. Worcestershire sauce
1/2 tsp. curry powder
1/2 tsp. cayenne pepper
1/8 tsp. salt

Cut the eggs in half lengthwise and remove the yolks. Place the yolks in a bowl. Mash the egg yolks with a fork. Add the mayonnaise, Worcestershire sauce, curry powder, cayenne pepper and salt to the egg yolks. Stir until well combined.

Spoon or pipe the egg yolks into the center of the egg whites. Place the eggs on a serving platter. Chill the eggs for 2 hours before serving. Store leftovers covered in the refrigerator up to 2 days.

Lemon Curry Deviled Eggs

Makes 16 servings

16 hard boiled eggs
1/2 cup sour cream
2 tbs. lemon juice
1/2 tsp. salt
1/2 tsp. paprika
1/2 tsp. ground mustard
1/2 tsp. curry powder
Dash of Worcestershire sauce

Cut the eggs in half lengthwise and remove the yolks. Place the yolks in a bowl. Mash the egg yolks with a fork. Add 1/3 cup sour cream, lemon juice, salt, paprika, ground mustard, curry powder and Worcestershire sauce to the egg yolks. Stir until well combined. Add the remaining sour cream if needed to make a creamy filling.

Spoon or pipe the egg yolks into the center of the egg whites. Place the eggs on a serving platter. Chill the eggs for 2 hours before serving. Store leftovers covered in the refrigerator up to 2 days.

Sante Fe Deviled Eggs

Makes 2 servings

2 hard boiled eggs, peeled
1 tbs. mayonnaise
1 tbs. canned chopped green chiles
1/2 tsp. chipotle pepper in adobo sauce
1/8 tsp. garlic salt
4 tsp. salsa
1 1/2 tsp. minced green onion
1 black olive, quartered

Cut the eggs in half lengthwise and remove the yolks. Add the yolks to a small bowl. Mash the yolks with a fork. Add the mayonnaise, green chiles, chipotle peppers and garlic salt to the yolks. Stir until combined.

Spoon the filling into the egg whites and place on a serving platter. Spoon the salsa, green onion and black olives over the top.

Texas Caviar Deviled Eggs

Makes 2 dozen

12 eggs
1/3 cup plain Greek yogurt
2 oz. cream cheese, softened
1 tbs. chopped fresh parsley
1 tsp. Dijon mustard
1/8 tsp. salt
3 tbs. chopped roasted red bell peppers
1 minced green onion
1 tbs. minced pickled jalapeno pepper
1 tbs. chopped fresh cilantro
1 tsp. dry Italian salad dressing mix
1/2 cup canned black eye peas, drained

Add the eggs to a large sauce pan over medium heat. Cover the eggs with water and bring the eggs to a full boil. Boil for 1 minute. Remove the pan from the heat and place a lid on the pan. Let the eggs sit for 10 minutes. Drain all the water from the pan.

Run cold water over the eggs until cool. Peel the eggs and slice in half lengthwise. Carefully remove the yolks and place in a small bowl. Mash the yolks with a fork. Add the yogurt, cream cheese, parsley, Dijon mustard, salt, red bell peppers, green onion, jalapeno pepper, cilantro and Italian salad dressing mix to the yolks. Stir until well combined. Spoon the filling into the egg white halves.

Spoon the black eye peas over the top of the eggs. Serve freshly made or refrigerate until chilled. Store the eggs in the refrigerator up to 2 days.

Ham Deviled Eggs

Makes 12 servings

6 hard boiled eggs, peeled
2 tbs. mayonnaise
2 tbs. cream cheese, softened
1 tsp. yellow prepared mustard
1 tsp. lemon juice
3 tbs. finely chopped cooked ham
2 1/4 tsp. finely minced fresh dill
1/2 tsp. caraway seeds
1/8 tsp. salt

Cut the eggs in half lengthwise and remove the yolks. Place the yolks in a bowl. Mash the egg yolks with a fork. Add the mayonnaise, cream cheese, mustard, lemon juice, ham, dill, caraway seeds and salt to the egg yolks. Stir until well combined.

Spoon or pipe the egg yolks into the center of the egg whites. Place the eggs on a serving platter. Chill the eggs for 2 hours before serving. Store leftovers covered in the refrigerator up to 2 days.

Chile Cheese Deviled Eggs

Makes 12 servings

12 hard boiled eggs, peeled
3 oz. pkg. cream cheese, softened
4 oz. can diced green chiles, drained
3 tbs. whole milk
1/4 tsp. salt

Cut the eggs in half lengthwise and remove the yolks. Place the yolks in a food processor. Add the cream cheese, green chiles, milk and salt to the food processor. Pulse until combined.

Spoon or pipe the egg yolks into the center of the egg whites. Place the eggs on a serving platter. Chill the eggs for 4 hours before serving. Store leftovers covered in the refrigerator up to 2 days.

Ham & Peach Deviled Eggs

Makes 2 dozen

12 eggs
1/3 cup plain Greek yogurt
2 oz. cream cheese, softened
1 tbs. chopped fresh parsley
1 tsp. Dijon mustard
1/8 tsp. salt
3 tbs. peach preserves
1/4 cup finely chopped cooked country ham
1 tsp. grated onion
1/2 tsp. apple cider vinegar
1/4 tsp. black pepper
1/2 cup finely chopped fresh peaches

Add the eggs to a large sauce pan over medium heat. Cover the eggs with water and bring the eggs to a full boil. Boil for 1 minute. Remove the pan from the heat and place a lid on the pan. Let the eggs sit for 10 minutes. Drain all the water from the pan.

Run cold water over the eggs until cool. Peel the eggs and slice in half lengthwise. Carefully remove the yolks and place in a small bowl. Mash the yolks with a fork. Add the yogurt, cream cheese, parsley, Dijon mustard, salt, peach preserves, ham, onion, apple cider vinegar and black pepper to the yolks. Stir until well combined. Spoon the filling into the egg white halves.

Spoon the fresh peaches over the top of the eggs. Serve freshly made or refrigerate until chilled. Store the eggs in the refrigerator up to 2 days.

Avocado and Ham Stuffed Eggs

Makes 2 dozen deviled eggs

12 hard boiled eggs, peeled
1 avocado, peeled and mashed
2 tbs. finely chopped onion
1 garlic clove, minced
2 tbs. mayonnaise
1 1/2 tbs. lime juice
1 tsp. Tabasco sauce
1/2 cup fresh tomato, finely chopped
6 oz. cooked country ham, thinly sliced

Cut the eggs in half lengthwise and remove the yolks. Place the yolks in a bowl. Mash the egg yolks with a fork. Add the mashed avocado, onion, garlic, mayonnaise, lime juice and Tabasco sauce to the egg yolks. Stir until well combined. Gently fold in the chopped tomato.

Spoon or pipe the egg yolks into the center of the egg whites. Place the eggs on a serving platter and place the ham strips over the top of each egg. Store leftovers covered in the refrigerator up to 2 days.

Sour Cream Herb Deviled Eggs

Makes 8 servings

8 hard boiled eggs, peeled
1/2 cup sour cream
3 tbs. chopped fresh chives
1 tbs. chopped fresh dill
2 tsp. white wine vinegar
1/4 tsp. salt
1/8 tsp. black pepper

Cut the eggs in half lengthwise and remove the yolks. Place the yolks in a bowl. Mash the egg yolks with a fork. Add 1/3 cup sour cream, chives, dill, white wine vinegar, salt and black pepper to the egg yolks. Stir until well combined. If the filling is too dry or you need a creamier filling, add the remaining sour cream.

Spoon or pipe the egg yolks into the center of the egg whites. Place the eggs on a serving platter. Chill the eggs for 4 hours before serving. Store leftovers covered in the refrigerator up to 2 days.

Brunch Crab Deviled Eggs

Makes 2 dozen

12 eggs
1/3 cup plain Greek yogurt
2 oz. cream cheese, softened
1 tbs. chopped fresh parsley
1 tsp. Dijon mustard
1/8 tsp. salt
1/2 cup cooked fresh lump crabmeat, chopped
2 tsp. fresh minced tarragon
12 tsp. grated lemon zest
1/4 tsp. black pepper

Add the eggs to a large sauce pan over medium heat. Cover the eggs with water and bring the eggs to a full boil. Boil for 1 minute. Remove the pan from the heat and place a lid on the pan. Let the eggs sit for 10 minutes. Drain all the water from the pan.

Run cold water over the eggs until cool. Peel the eggs and slice in half lengthwise. Carefully remove the yolks and place in a small bowl. Mash the yolks with a fork. Add the yogurt, cream cheese, parsley, Dijon mustard, salt, crab, tarragon, lemon zest and black pepper to the yolks. Stir until well combined. Spoon the filling into the egg white halves. Serve freshly made or refrigerate until chilled. Store the eggs in the refrigerator up to 2 days.

Crab Deviled Eggs

Makes 2 dozen

12 hard boiled eggs, peeled
6 oz. flaked cooked crabmeat
1/2 cup mayonnaise
1 green onion, finely chopped
1 tbs. finely chopped celery
1 tbs. finely chopped green bell pepper
2 tsp. Dijon mustard
1 tsp. minced fresh parsley
1/2 tsp. salt
1/8 tsp. black pepper
3 dashes Tabasco sauce
3 dashes Worcestershire sauce

Cut the eggs in half lengthwise and remove the yolks. Place the yolks in a bowl. Mash the egg yolks with a fork. Add the crabmeat, mayonnaise, green onion, celery, green bell pepper, Dijon mustard, parsley, salt, black pepper, Tabasco sauce and Worcestershire sauce to the egg yolks. Stir until well combined.

Spoon or pipe the egg yolks into the center of the egg whites. Place the eggs on a serving platter. Chill the eggs for 4 hours before serving. Store leftovers covered in the refrigerator up to 2 days.

Potato Stuffed Eggs

Makes 2 dozen

The use of instant potato flakes make the filling heartier and smooth. It is very good.

1 dozen hard boiled eggs, peeled
3/4 cup mayonnaise
1 tbs. Dijon mustard
1/4 tsp. salt
1/4 tsp. black pepper
1/2 cup instant potato flakes

Cut the eggs in half lengthwise and remove the yolks. Place the yolks in a food processor. Add the mayonnaise, Dijon mustard, salt, black pepper and potato flakes to the food processor. Pulse until smooth.

Turn the food processor off and spoon the filling into the egg whites. Place the deviled eggs on a platter. Cover the platter and chill the eggs at least 8 hours before serving.

Dill Deviled Eggs

Makes 1 dozen

6 hard boiled eggs
1/4 cup mayonnaise
1 tsp. white wine vinegar
1 tsp. Dijon mustard
1/2 tsp. dried dill
1/4 tsp. garlic powder
1/8 tsp. salt

Peel the eggs and slice in half lengthwise. Carefully remove the yolks and place in a small bowl. Mash the yolks with a fork. Add the mayonnaise, white wine vinegar, Dijon mustard, dill, garlic powder and salt to the yolks. Stir until well combined. Spoon the filling into the egg white halves. Serve freshly made or refrigerate until chilled. Store the eggs in the refrigerator up to 2 days.

Thousand Island Deviled Eggs

This dish is so easy and this is my husband's favorite deviled eggs.

Makes 12 eggs

6 hard boiled eggs, peeled
2 bacon slices, cooked and crumbled
1/3 cup bottled Thousand Island dressing
24 small red pimento strips

Cut the eggs in half lengthwise and remove the yolks. Place the yolks in a bowl. Mash the egg yolks with a fork. Add the bacon and Thousand Island dressing to the yolks. Stir until well combined.

Spoon or pipe the egg yolks into the center of the egg whites. Place the eggs on a serving platter. Place 2 red pimento strips over each egg. Serve the eggs freshly made or chilled. Store leftovers covered in the refrigerator up to 2 days.

Bacon and Chive Potato Stuffed Eggs

Makes 2 dozen

1 dozen hard boiled eggs, peeled
3/4 cup mayonnaise
1 tbs. Dijon mustard
1/4 tsp. salt
1/4 tsp. black pepper
1/2 cup instant potato flakes
2/3 cup cooked bacon, crumbled
3 tbs. dill or sweet pickle relish
1/4 cup chopped chives

Cut the eggs in half lengthwise and remove the yolks. Place the yolks in a food processor. Add the mayonnaise, Dijon mustard, salt, black pepper, potato flakes, bacon, pickle relish and chives to the food processor. Pulse until smooth.

Turn the food processor off and spoon the filling into the egg whites. Place the deviled eggs on a platter. Cover the platter and chill the eggs at least 8 hours before serving.

Shrimp & Green Onion Potato Stuffed Eggs

Makes 2 dozen

1 dozen hard boiled eggs, peeled
3/4 cup mayonnaise
1 tbs. Dijon mustard
1/4 tsp. salt
1/4 tsp. black pepper
1/2 cup instant potato flakes
3/4 lb. cooked shrimp, finely chopped
2 tbs. prepared horseradish
6 green onions, minced

Cut the eggs in half lengthwise and remove the yolks. Place the yolks in a food processor. Add the mayonnaise, Dijon mustard, salt, black pepper, potato flakes, shrimp, horseradish and green onions to the food processor. Process until smooth.

Turn the food processor off and spoon the filling into the egg whites. Place the deviled eggs on a platter. Cover the platter and chill the eggs at least 8 hours before serving.

Spinach and Bacon Stuffed Eggs

Makes 2 dozen

1 dozen hard boiled eggs, peeled
3/4 cup mayonnaise
1 tbs. Dijon mustard
1/4 tsp. salt
1/4 tsp. black pepper
1 cup cooked spinach, well drained
5 bacon slices, cooked and crumbled
3 green onions, minced
1/3 cup instant potato flakes

Cut the eggs in half lengthwise and remove the yolks. Place the yolks in a food processor. Add the mayonnaise, Dijon mustard, salt, black pepper, spinach, bacon, green onions and potato flakes to the food processor. Process until smooth.

Turn the food processor off and spoon the filling into the egg whites. Place the deviled eggs on a platter. Cover the platter and chill the eggs at least 8 hours before serving.

Spinach Deviled Eggs

Makes 2 dozen

12 hard boiled eggs
1/4 cup mayonnaise
2 tbs. white vinegar
2 tbs. unsalted butter, softened
1 tbs. granulated sugar
1/2 tsp. black pepper
1/4 tsp. salt
1/2 cup frozen chopped spinach, thawed & patted dry
4 bacon slices, cooked & crumbled

Cut the eggs in half lengthwise and remove the yolks. Place the yolks in a bowl. Mash the egg yolks with a fork. Add the mayonnaise, white vinegar, butter, granulated sugar, black pepper, salt, spinach and bacon to the yolks. Stir until well combined.

Spoon or pipe the egg yolks into the center of the egg whites. Place the eggs on a serving platter. Serve the eggs freshly made or chilled. Store leftovers covered in the refrigerator. These eggs are best eaten the day they are made.

German Pickled Eggs

Makes 1 dozen

2 cups cider vinegar
1 cup granulated sugar
1/2 cup water
2 tbs. prepared mustard
1 tbs. salt
1 tbs. celery seed
1 tbs. mustard seed
6 whole cloves
2 onions, thinly sliced
12 hard boiled eggs, peeled

In a large sauce pan over medium heat, add the cider vinegar, granulated sugar, water, prepared mustard, salt, celery seed, mustard seed and cloves. Bring to a boil and reduce the heat to low. Place a lid on the pan and simmer for 10 minutes. Remove the pan from the heat and cool completely before using.

Add the onions and eggs to a large glass jar with a lid. Pour the vinegar over the eggs until they are completely covered. Place the lid on the jar. Refrigerate for 24 hours before serving. Will keep for 1 week in the refrigerator.

Eggs, Omelets & Frittatas

Eggs, Omelets & Frittatas, cont'd

Florentine Mushroom Omelet, 37
Baked Vegetable Omelet, 38
Cream Cheese & Chive Omelet, 38
Monterey Jack Omelets With Bacon Avocado Salsa, 39
Baked Rolled Vegetable Omelet, 40
Asparagus Crab Omelets, 41
Italian Pizza Omelet, 42
Goat Cheese & Tomato Omelet, 43
Oven Baked Denver Omelet, 43
French Potato Omelets, 44
Spinach Red Pepper Omelet, 44
Spinach & Cheese Omelet, 45
Mushroom Omelet, 45
Deluxe Ham Omelet, 46
Cheddar, Ham & Green Onion Baked Omelet, 46
Hot & Spicy Omelet, 47
Spicy Bacon Omelet, 47
Southwestern Omelet, 48
Asian Dinner Omelet, 49
Strawberry Banana Omelet, 50
Strawberry Bliss Omelet, 51
Ham & Avocado Egg Scramble, 52
Spinach Mushroom Scrambled Eggs, 52
Tex Mex Scramble, 53
Tex Mex Migas, 53
Cream Cheese Basil Scrambled Eggs, 54
Curry Egg Scramble, 54
Calico Scrambled Eggs, 55
Bacon & Potato Scrambled Eggs, 55
Southwest Tortilla Scramble, 56
Green Onion & Cream Cheese Scrambled Eggs, 56
Haystack Eggs, 57
Bacon Cheddar Egg Scramble, 57
Mexican Scrambled Eggs, 58
Salmon Scramble, 58
Corn Scrambled Eggs, 59
Mexican Corn Scramble, 59
Savory Topped Bacon Scrambled Eggs, 60
Mushroom Onion Breakfast Scramble, 61
Sausage Breakfast Hash, 62
Barbecue Chicken Polenta With Fried Eggs, 63
Huevos Rancheros With Tomatillo Sauce, 64
Denver Scrambled Egg Tostadas, 64
Vegetable Scrambled Eggs, 65
Garden Scrambled Eggs, 65

Quiches

Crustless Bacon Mushroom Quiche, 67
Bacon Quiche, 67
Canadian Bacon & Onion Quiche, 68
Caramelized Onion Quiche, 69
Roasted Sweet Potato & Onion Quiche, 70
Quesadilla Quiche, 71
Mushroom Asparagus Quiche, 72
Kentucky Hot Brown Quiche, 73
Bacon Vegetable Quiche, 74
Ham & Bacon Quiche, 75
Mini Ham Quiches, 76
Ham & Cheddar Quiche, 76
Turkey Swiss Quiche, 77
Asparagus Quiche, 78
Smoked Sausage Crustless Quiche, 78
Green Vegetable Quiche, 79
Pear Pecan Sausage Quiche, 80
Southwestern Quiche, 81
South Of The Border Breakfast Quiche, 82
Cheesy Sausage Quiche, 83
Crab Quiche Bake, 83
Golden Corn Quiche, 84
Broccoli Hashbrown Quiche, 84
Cheesy Vegetable Quiche, 85
Cream Cheese Spinach Quiche, 86
Pepperoni Spinach Quiche, 87
Bacon Quiche Cups, 88
Cheddar Egg Custard Cups, 88
Bacon Gruyere Puff Pastry Quiche Cups, 89
Broccoli Quiche Crepe Cups, 90
Savory Omelet Cups, 91

Sandwiches & Salads

Toasted Scrambled Egg Sandwiches, 138
Ham, Egg & Cheese Breakfast Sandwich, 139
Bacon, Egg & Muenster Cheese Bagels, 139
Scrambled Egg & Fontina Sandwiches, 140
Ham & Cheese Sauce Topped English Muffins, 140
Wild Mushroom & Cheddar Sandwiches, 141
Grilled Bacon & Egg Biscuit, 142
Anytime Bacon, Egg & Cheese Sandwiches, 142
Prosciutto, Cheddar & Egg Breakfast Biscuits, 143
Italian Sausage & Egg Croissants, 144
Omelet Croissants, 145
Spicy Scrambled Egg Sandwiches, 146
Ham Breakfast Wraps, 146
Fried Egg & Pancetta Sandwiches, 147
Scrambled Egg Muffin Sliders, 148
Mexican Breakfast Burritos, 149
Green Chili Breakfast Burritos, 149
Sausage, Egg & Cheese Burritos, 150
Sausage Monterey Jack Breakfast Burritos, 151
Egg Baguette Bake, 152
Tortilla Wrapped Asparagus Omelet, 153
Spanish Brunch Wraps, 154
Italian Sausage & Egg Breakfast Burrito, 155
Breakfast Egg & Sausage Quesadillas, 156
Huevos Rancheros Quesadillas, 157
Scotch Eggs, 157
Farmer Egg Salad, 158
Egg Salad Sandwich Filling, 159
Ham & Egg Salad Sandwich Filling, 159
Shrimp Egg Salad, 160
Crab Egg Cracker Spread, 160

Deviled Eggs

Cajun Spiced Deviled Eggs, 162
Smoked Salmon & Cream Cheese Deviled Eggs, 162
Pecan Stuffed Deviled Eggs, 163
Spicy Sweet Deviled Eggs, 163
Tex Mex Deviled Eggs, 164
Bacon Stuffed Eggs, 164
Blue Cheese Deviled Eggs, 165
Cream Cheese Yogurt Deviled Eggs, 165
Green Pea Deviled Eggs, 166
Mexican Deviled Eggs, 166
Shrimp and Bacon Deviled Eggs, 167
Shrimp Remoulade Deviled Eggs, 167
Smoky Pimento Cheese Deviled Eggs, 168
Spicy Deviled Eggs, 168
Cilantro Tuna Salad Deviled Eggs, 169
Deluxe Deviled Eggs, 169
Creole Shrimp Deviled Eggs, 170
Curry Deviled Eggs, 170
Lemon Curry Deviled Eggs, 171
Sante Fe Deviled Eggs, 171
Texas Caviar Deviled Eggs, 172
Ham Deviled Eggs, 173
Chile Cheese Deviled Eggs, 173
Ham & Peach Deviled Eggs, 174
Avocado and Ham Stuffed Eggs, 175
Sour Cream Herb Deviled Eggs, 175
Brunch Crab Deviled Eggs, 176
Crab Deviled Eggs, 177
Potato Stuffed Eggs, 177
Dill Deviled Eggs, 178
Thousand Island Deviled Eggs, 178
Bacon and Chive Potato Stuffed Eggs, 179
Shrimp & Green Onion Potato Stuffed Eggs, 179
Spinach and Bacon Stuffed Eggs, 180
Spinach Deviled Eggs, 180
German Pickled Eggs, 181

ABOUT THE AUTHOR

Lifelong southerner who lives in Bowling Green, KY. Priorities in life are God, family and pets. I love to cook, garden and feed most any stray animal that walks into my yard. I love old cookbooks and cookie jars. Huge NBA fan who loves to spend hours watching basketball games. Enjoy cooking for family and friends and hosting parties and reunions. Can't wait each year to build gingerbread houses for the kids.